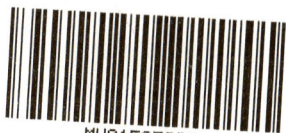

BWB Texts

Short books on big subjects from great New Zealand writers

Ko Taranaki Te Maunga

RACHEL BUCHANAN

Published in 2018 by Bridget Williams Books Limited, PO Box 12474, Wellington 6144, New Zealand, www.bwb.co.nz, info@bwb.co.nz. Reprinted 2018 and 2019.

ISBN 9781988545288 (Paperback), ISBN 9781988545257 (EPUB)
ISBN 9781988545264 (KINDLE), ISBN 9781988545271 (PDF)
DOI 10.7810/9781988545288

A catalogue record for this book is available from the National Library of New Zealand. Kei te pātenga raraunga o Te Puna Mātauranga o Aotearoa te whakarārangi o tēnei pukapuka.

Acknowledgements
The publisher acknowledges the ongoing support provided by the Bridget Williams Books Publishing Trust and Creative New Zealand.

Publisher: Tom Rennie
Editor: Jane Parkin
Cover and internal design: Neil Pardington Design
Typesetter: Tina Delceg
Printer: Printlink, Wellington

CONTENTS

1. TIME ZONES

When I heard in 2017 that the New Zealand government was going up to Parihaka to apologise for the invasion and ransacking of the pā, my first thought was: Oh no, not again! I totted up how many times the government had already said sorry for te pāhua (the plunder). I thought it would have to be eight or nine by now. I was sorry too, but for different reasons.

Parihaka, a pan-tribal pā in the centre of Taranaki iwi rohe, is halfway between the mountain, Taranaki, and the sea. It was set up in 1866 by Te Whiti o Rongomai and Tohu Kākahi, two brilliant political and spiritual leaders who used non-violence to resist land confiscations and colonisation. In less than two decades Parihaka became the nation's biggest and best-organised Māori community, but on 5 November 1881, fifteen hundred police and volunteers, led by Native Minister John Bryce, invaded the pā. They were met by singing, skipping children, women carrying baskets of bread baked for the soldiers, and two thousand five hundred unarmed people sitting quietly on the marae. The Riot Act was read, obviously. Bryce demanded a response to the proclamation: would the people at Parihaka accept the 'large and ample' reserves it had promised to set aside for them? Would they submit to the law of the Queen? No answer. An hour went by. Then the Minister ordered Te Whiti's arrest. Next was Tohu, and finally Hīroki, a man alleged to have murdered a surveyor.

In the days that followed, police and soldiers raped women, stole family heirlooms, destroyed crops, pulled down homes and sacred buildings, and evicted fifteen hundred residents. For the next five years, armed troops occupied Parihaka. The invasion, a culmination of twenty years of military and legislative violence in Taranaki, is an especially low episode in the nation's history and since 1991 governments have made various attempts to atone for it.

Fewer than fifty people live at the pā now and hundreds visited on 9 June 2017 for He Puanga Haeata, the Parihaka–Crown Reconciliation Ceremony, the latest and most elaborate attempt at making amends, and one that fell outside the Treaty of Waitangi settlement process. The ceremony was widely covered. The reports were detailed, sensitive and useful.

My favourite coverage was a photograph published on the RNZ website. It depicted carver Rangi Kipa spinning a pūrēhua (bull roarer) 'to gather the spirits ahead of the Crown's arrival for the apology'. Kipa was facing the mountain, a perfect blue cone rising up from the volcanic green. Taranaki was demure. His snow-capped head was exposed but he wore a piupiu made from clouds around his middle.

I looked at that picture on my computer at the University of Melbourne Archives where I was working. My stomach cramped. Pain, regret, fear and sorrow stirred, then hardened inside me. I was up the mountain, scrambling through the bush, trying to keep up with Dad. He had gone off the track. We'd lost the group. The supplejack whipped against my face and arms. Rope burn. Wheezing. Sore feet. Hungry too. Now, in Melbourne, I was so far away. Why hadn't I made the trip back for the ceremony? Why hadn't I taken Mum and Dad with me? The coverage and commentary suggested that this Parihaka apology really did seem to be a lot better than some of the earlier ones. My scepticism had been misplaced.

It's a strange claim to make, but when it comes to Parihaka, I'm an expert in the business of being sorry.

This knowledge is a byproduct of my doctorate on the historiography of Parihaka. I began my PhD in 2001. I wanted to track a history of history-making about the place from 1881 until the early twenty-first century. Te Miringa Hōhaia and the Parihaka Pā trustees had just partnered with City Gallery Wellington and Victoria University Press to show and publish *Parihaka: The Art of Passive Resistance*, an astonishing exhibition and accompanying catalogue. It seemed to me that the invasion of Parihaka had become an important but also tenuous foundational moment in oral, written, visual and performative historical storytelling in New Zealand. Why? Parihaka was a place and an event that could be lost and found, over and over. It moved into view, then disappeared, just like the mountain.

My first baby arrived when I was eight months into my candidature. In 2002 Lily Arapera was my companion on a research trip back to New Zealand. She was dribbling and rolling about in a playpen at the Waitangi Tribunal offices when I read a few interesting papers in the archive generated by the Tribunal's epic Taranaki hearings (thirteen separate sittings spread out over five years, thirty-three substantial research reports, dozens of individual claimant testimonies). An archivist had listed the papers as part of the records generated by the sixth Taranaki hearing. One document was an angry letter the Parihaka Pā trustees wrote to the Minister of Justice, Doug Graham, in 1992. The subject line was: 're apology for Parihaka'. The letter stayed with me as I wrote my doctorate and then rewrote the doctorate so it could become a book. In late 2009, my parents and Lily came with me to Parihaka to present the manuscript of *The Parihaka Album: Lest We Forget* to Te Miringa Hōhaia and others at Te Pae Pae, one of Parihaka's three marae. 'Bread and Breath', an account of this journey, co-authored with Maria Tumarkin, was later published in *Australian Humanities Review.*

Mahara Okeroa, a former Labour Party MP who represented Te Tai Tonga Māori electorate from 1999 to 2008, launched *The Parihaka Album* in early 2010 at the old Port Nicholson Settlement Trust offices behind the Wellington Railway Station. Mahara grew up at Parihaka. I did not know him, but I had met his mother Ngahina when I stayed at Te Niho, another of Parihaka's marae, as a schoolgirl in 1981, the one hundredth anniversary of the invasion.

The year the book was out I was also invited to speak at a symposium on apology and historical injustice at Waikato University. I asked Te Miringa what he thought, and he encouraged me to take on the challenging topic of Parihaka apologies and consider what, if anything, they might mean.

As I went on, my work gathered an exciting

energy and my ideas shifted. With the guidance of many others, my focus turned from thinking about apologies to thinking about whakamā (shame). Finally, after a rigorous peer review, the essay that grew from the original symposium paper and subsequent talks was published in 2012 in the little-known *Te Pouhere Kōrero*, the journal of the Māori Historians Association.[1] *Te Pouhere Kōrero* is something of an underground publication. Not widely known but full of riches.

My essay was called 'Beating Shame: Parihaka and the Very Long Sorry'. It had my name at the top, but my writing was a vehicle for collective effort and knowledge. The essay was an engine. It had made things happen. As I reflected on the reconciliation ceremony, the engine sparked. The work wasn't finished. Some of the people who had helped me with it were dead. My dad would soon be dead too. He had terminal cancer. His life was now measured in days and weeks.

Death is labour, just like birth. Both events resist schedules. They stretch time into new shapes. You are woken in the dark by a cry. The baby needs another feed. You tug your hand off that sticky moment and it lands on another, far worse. 'Morphine,' the voice says. 'Morphine, morphine.' A figure lurches into the doorway, one hand on the wall, the other clutching a tokotoko. It's 2 a.m. The fridge light glows blue. The vials are inside the

ClickClack container next to half an avocado on a plate. Subcutaneous. Dongle. Nozinam. Morphine. Thin arm, skin grey. Head down. Panting. Dad.

I remembered the birth plan I had written before Lily came. All my wishes and instructions, my airy tone, my mention of therapeutic massage and low lighting, the haughty way I placed the word 'pain' in sentences, as if 'pain' was just another word, rather than an entire language that I did not know how to speak. The baby was two weeks late. The induction drugs pumped the new language right in under my skin. Instant knowledge. Prep to PhD in a flash. The clock in the hospital room still beat in time with the old world. It said five minutes had passed. The pain said an eternity. I had to escape ooze time. I looked at my arm. I knew what to do. I would unzip my skin and step out of my body.

Now death was due. It was no more convenient than birth. There was the waiting for signs, then the bouts of spurious labour. Dad said he was on the runway. The departure time remained a mystery, although several announcements had been made. 'If he can use his mobile and ring you up to say he is dying, he's not dying,' a nurse said to my brother.

I inhabited all the different time zones at once, the places where my family lived, the phases of my life, the phases of my children's lives. The clocks ticked inside me. Melbourne time. Wellington time. Berlin time. Childhood time. Teenager time.

Middle-age time. Old-age time. Taranaki time. Mountain time. Uncharted territory time. Deep-space time. Catholic time. The dying Dad time.

The alarm went off on the Taranaki clock. The essay could be my proxy. I emailed Tom Rennie, the publisher of the BWB Texts series, and sent him a scan of my 'beating shame' piece (from *Te Pouhere Kōrero*) and waited hopefully. Then, a Fairfax journalist based in New Plymouth tracked me down and asked if she could interview me for a feature story she was working on about the Parihaka reconciliation. She mentioned the essay on shame. I was surprised she knew of it. I noticed an opinion piece by Dennis Ngāwhare-Pounamu. I was even more surprised to see my shame essay was referenced in there as well. This underground piece of writing certainly seemed to be getting around.

I googled the title and discovered Parihaka had published a pdf of my essay on its website (Parihaka. maori.nz). No one had asked for my permission but I was glad my work had been useful. My essay was categorised as a 'Key Document for Reconciliation Process', and had been published below a report on how to improve sewage treatment at Parihaka and another report on the state of internal roads. This was a high honour indeed. My work was part of the critical infrastructure for repair.

The book pitch went on the back burner. Each

day was a struggle to resist two mighty but opposing forces that were drawing in closer.

One force was Dad. The other was Australian-born feminist Germaine Greer. For the past two years I had been curating the archive that Greer had spent fifty years amassing. The University of Melbourne had bought the collection from her, and I was in charge of a team of archivists who were cataloguing, processing and promoting five hundred boxes of letters, manuscripts, photos, videos, books, news clippings, diaries, car registration papers, old passports, cassettes as well as born-digital material: one of the biggest and juiciest collections of personal papers in Australia. We called our workplace Greer Town. I loved the job but it was not without challenges, one of which was the need to communicate regularly with the archive's creator, often on topics of some sensitivity.

Greer lives in Essex, England. One of her pet sayings is: Never apologise. Never explain. The texture of that philosophy is similar to the texture of a reinforced- steel security door. There's not a lot of give in it.

I kept a framed photograph of maunga Taranaki on my desk and I would look at him in the mornings and ask for strength. Sometimes I'd utter a karakia to help me through. *Whakataka te hau ki te uru, Whakataka te hau ki te tonga* …

On International Women's Day 2017, I chaired a

public event in Melbourne called 'Germaine Greer Meets the Archivists'. Five archivists, including me, gave short performances about a particular part of the archive, and then Greer responded. There was time for a Q and A at the end. Many hands shot up. The questions were tough, but Greer did not step back or even stand her ground. She stepped forward into every punch. The air crackled with danger. I made a few jokes to defuse the tension. At the end of the night, I felt a survivor's exhilaration. I was keen to hear what my daughters thought.

'Germaine Greer is just like Pa Leo,' Lily said.

I was awed by her ability to discern a connection between two such seemingly opposite individuals.

Dad – Pa Leo as his mokopuna called him – was only a couple of years younger than Greer. Both were intellectual, radical and unyielding in many of their views. Both had been raised Catholics. Both had photographic memories. Both venerated literature. Both held a special fondness for the early modern period. Most significantly, both were meticulous record-keepers. They had arranged and rearranged their papers many times over the years, each demonstrating a keen grasp of a fact too often overlooked – that keeping records is a subversive thing to do, a political act, a shout out to the future. Record-keeping is an insurance against death, like cryogenics.

In his end-of-life frenzy, Dad was even creating

records about what he hoped would come next. The Heaven Project, he called this activity. 'You know my views, Rachel. The afterlife is more important to me than this one.' He had written Lily a letter on the topic. The handwritten original (eight pages) and several other photocopies were stored in his filing cabinet in the apartment he shared with Mum at Wellington's Village at the Park, along with multiple versions of his instructions for his send-off.

All this was a distraction from the non-celestial realm, where Dad and Mum still lived. When Dad went, what would happen to Mum? Mary had dementia and Dad was her carer. It was a role he would not give up even though he was no longer capable of it. Their fifty-year marriage was like the *Titanic*, a luxury liner that was taking in water fast. My sisters and brothers in Wellington were flat out trying to keep the vessel afloat. I bobbed back and forth across the ditch.

In Melbourne I managed the team of archivists. Our days were occupied with preserving the memory of women's liberation and the radical thinking and work that flowed from it. We wrote thousands of words of metadata about the archive. We wrote instructions on access management to be read by future colleagues who had not yet been born. My workplace was focused on the perpetual. An archive is a thing of 'endless duration', a collection of documents scooped up from oblivion.

In Wellington, the stress of Dad's illness sped Mum's memory loss. A thought would form, a bubble, then pop! Mary's words disappeared into the fog. My mother would reach for the thought and it would dance just beyond her fingers. She pounded her fists on the table. 'Delete, delete,' she would say, and make a cutting motion in the air. Mary is a mother of eight. I'm the oldest. As soon as she got pregnant with me, she stopped work as a teacher. And that was it for money jobs. Her husband would become a medical specialist (paediatrician) and he did the paid work. Women's liberation did not change Mary's life. It barely registered. Motherhood was her life; it was the source and evidence of her creative energy, and the place where she expended it. As well as Dad, she mothered her biological children, two foster children, several of her children's friends, and many of her eleven younger siblings.

Leo was aware of women's liberation. His view of the movement and the feminisms that followed was mostly one of amused disdain and dismissal, although when challenged he could be virulent in his criticisms of women's right to obtain a safe abortion, for example, or even to use a childcare centre so she could do paid work outside the home. He was unable to accept that my relationship with Mike – we've been together for twenty-four years and have three children – did not need to be legitimised by either church or state via marriage. He decided to raise this topic when he was on his deathbed in hospital in late 2016. He suggested that marriage provided a better environment for children. I was not going to stand for it: my last conversation with Dad would not be one in which he suggested I had failed my kids. In the argument that ensued, Dad even tried to flip over his food tray. His cup of broth spilt and tiny bits of carrot sloshed about on the plastic surface. 'If you are going to be like that,' Dad said, 'you can just bugger off!'

His Catholicism was intense, and it provided a practical as well as spiritual framework for his life and my mother's. For many years, my parents went to Mass first thing every morning. They were church hoppers. St Mary of the Angels; St Patrick's in Kilbirnie; 'Hogwarts', which was Dad's name for the old Apostolic Nunciature of the Holy See in Lyall Bay. I respected their faith but did not share it.

The Māori world was where he and I could connect. That connection had started back in 1986 when we both enrolled – unbeknownst to the other – in a six-week total-immersion te reo course at Kuratini in Wellington. I was a teenager. Dad was the superintendent of Masterton Hospital.

We both enjoyed the intrigues and scandals, the intensity, the rituals, the spontaneity, the emphasis on the face to face, the unexpected drama of various hui, the power plays of the Māori world. I skirted the edges because of who I am, how I was raised and where I live. Even so, I could see this world operated quite separately from the ordinary New Zealand one. It was governed by different rules and ruled by a different set of people. All these important events occurred in this Māori world, the Taranaki Māori world, but the rest of the country crept on, oblivious. I don't know if Dad felt the same way and I can't ask him now.

The last time I spoke with Leo was on a Sunday afternoon. I got through to him in his bed in the hospital wing at Village at the Park, his ancestral land. Even then he was still head of the trust that oversaw the place on behalf of the Wellington Tenths Trust, the Te Ātiawa-Taranaki owners of the site in Berhampore where Athletic Park used to be. Dad's voice was weak. He said he was waiting for Finch (a family friend) to arrive but he had lost his watch. He had looked everywhere for it. 'I'm groggy,' he said. 'I need to find my watch. I can't find it. Where is it?'

Two days later, his time was up. I was waiting in the departure lounge at Melbourne when I got the call. Back in Wellington I instinctively looked for Dad and Mum. They always met me. They would sit side by side in their raincoats, jerseys and scarves, faces turned towards the sliding doors. Mum in her beanie, Dad in some other sort of hat, often a black trilby or an old baseball cap emblazoned with a drug company logo. First it was just me, then I would come back with a mokopuna. Then another. Then a third, snuggled in against my chest in a sling. As I got older, I found it harder to look at their eager, vulnerable faces because I saw my own future written there, the time when I will be the one waiting for my own children to return to me.

Once, Mum and Dad waited for three-and-a-half hours. That was in October 2009, when I came back to take the proofs of my book up to Parihaka. Lily was with me and our plane had been diverted via Auckland because the weather in Wellington was so foul that the pilot ('an Australian pilot', as one passenger said in a loud voice) was unable to land. We refueled and the Australian pilot decided to turn round and give Wellington another go, and this time he touched down. By the time we got through Customs, it was after eight. We needed to get up to Taranaki that night. Dad did the first spell up to Foxton, then I said I'd take the wheel. The rain was coming straight for us, and so were the monstrous milk tankers. They missed the driver's side by a whisker and sprayed the windscreen with blinding gritty mist. I was too scared to drive, so Dad took over and navigated us safely through that long winding stretch into Whanganui and beyond.

We stayed at his favourite place, the Auto Lodge

Motor Inn on Devon Street, New Plymouth, and the next night Tony and Ann Ruakere took us out for dinner across the road at Marbles Buffet. It was an all-you-can-eat place, and the all included ice cream from a snow-freeze machine and four different types of potatoes, all fried. Who was happier about these options? Lily or Leo? I'm still not sure. When we got to Te Pae Pae at Parihaka, Tony's brother Lindsay McLeod was waiting. He would come on with us. He called my daughter Arapera and greeted her in his elegant Māori. He pointed to a house on the hill. 'I was raised there,' he said.

Lindsay has passed away now too, and Tony was too unwell to make the trip down for Dad's tangi. I spent much of the week after Dad's death in his and my mother's apartment, appraising his personal papers. The top drawer of the cabinet held papers relating to Māori land and whakapapa. Dad's handwritten labels said: Wellington Tenths, Polhill Gully, Papakainga, Taranaki Iwi, Port Nicholson Block, Maori Land Affairs, Te Reo, Te Atiawa iwi, Orimupiko, PKW, Te Hapu. When I looked in the folders, I found copies of my research papers and talks filed next to Dad's material. We had worked together for years, really. Tākuta tāngata (doctor people), as Mahara Okeroa once called us.

The folders contained records kept by my great-grandmother Hannah, my grandmother Rawinia, and my dad. The first records were from between the wars. Here was eighty years of non-violent protest against colonisation. This was our whānau's passive resistance. These records documented their dispossession, but with time had become a force for the exact opposite. Taranaki maunga watched my work. He was part of the letterhead on Taranaki Māori Trust Board stationery, a white feather slung across his chest.

Alone in that hot little apartment, I realised that through keeping these records, my grandmothers and father had expressed a deep love not just for me and all their other uri (descendants) but also for their own tūpuna, even if they did not know their names or where they came from.

Then in January 2018 BWB responded. They were keen to publish. My Melbourne contract was coming to an end and it was time to return to Taranaki.

2. PAPER MOUNTAIN

Almost fifty years after the Waitangi Tribunal was set up and twenty-eight years after the first modern Treaty settlement (about Waitomo Caves), it is dispiriting to accept that some – perhaps many – people still do not know anything about Parihaka and the Taranaki wars. A brief history is needed here.

Knowing this, but uncertain where and how to start, I got up from my desk and went outside to look for the perfect stone, something flat and smooth. I often put stones in my pocket as a souvenir of somewhere special. I've got Taranaki stones here in Melbourne and I've got Wellington stones too. I like to rub them when I'm unsure. I found a nice round one and warmed it up in my palm. Then I flicked the stone out over the water and watched it skip.

In 1866, Taranaki leaders Te Whiti o Rongomai and Tohu Kākahi established Parihaka as a final refuge for Māori who had been dispossessed by the wars of colonisation and the confiscations that were part of those wars.

That sentence is the stone and the past is the lake. From a Taranaki perspective, one of the things the sentence skips over is the wars before the wars. The violent upheavals of the 1820s and 1830s – like many other significant events that occurred before the Treaty was signed in 1840 – are outside the scope of the history created and narrated by the Waitangi Tribunal and Office of Treaty Settlements. I find these times hard to understand too, even though they shaped the lives of many of my relatives.

Before the wars with the Crown, Taranaki was hollowed out by the cycle of fighting and retribution that began with the 1821 arrival of a large tāua (war party) from the far north, and from Waikato and Maniapoto. Some people were taken prisoner, some were slaughtered, and others fled south. These sentences also skim the surface of particular horrors. In the 1820s Taranaki people from many hapū hid at an ancient pā site, Te Maru, about 1500 metres up the western side of Mt Taranaki. Waikato found them, and hundreds of people were either killed or enslaved. Even without guns, we Taranaki people did our share of killing and mocking. In 1831 Waikato took retribution for an earlier humiliation when Te Ātiawa had imprisoned hundreds of Tainui warriors at Pukerangiora Pā, built on cliffs 100 metres above the Waitara River. A war party laid siege to Pukerangiora and many of the trapped people decided to jump off the cliffs rather than be butchered or enslaved. As many as twelve hundred were killed or captured.

Others fled to Te Namu Pā. In 1833, Taranaki iwi (or Taranaki Tūturu, as our iwi is also called) warrior Wiremu Kīngi Te Matakātea and about eighty men and their families holed up at Te Namu, a rock on the headland at Ōpunake, and prepared for a final battle against Waikato. Te Matakātea (clear eyed) had the only musket and his deadly accurate shot earned him his name. After a long siege, he and his people beat eight hundred invaders by pelting them with stones.

To escape the carnage, my closest relatives fled their homes around Orimupiko at Ōpunake and walked south to Waikanae, then kept going down the gorge to Te Whanganui-a-Tara. They settled at Te Aro, the pā that still lies beneath Taranaki Street, and they grew their veges up the hill at Pukeahu, the place that became known as Mount Cook, and they caught their fish in the harbour, beetling about on waka with their relatives. One of their relatives, Minarapa Te Rangihatuake, taught them how to pray, and they helped him build a raupō church, the first one in the region. Minarapa, a captive first of

Waikato, then of Ngā Puhi, had become a Wesleyan lay preacher in the Hokianga, and in 1839 he went south to bring the Gospel to Te Whanganui-a-Tara. And there they all were when the first New Zealand Company ships sailed into the harbour with their cargo of adventurous people who were eager to occupy the land they had been sold, by lottery, in England.

The land was cut up like a cake. We were kindly granted one piece and the company got the other nine. But even that one piece was too much. It was nibbled away at, chewed over, snatched. The Wellington Tenths Trust administers the crumbs.

The Wellington City Council built Taranaki Street over Te Aro Pā. A paradox: the name of the street that wiped out our kāinga recalls the existence of the kāinga.

When my father Leo was a child in post-Second World War Wellington, his grandmother Hannah Bramley (née Wallace) used to take him to a coffee shop near where the Oaks complex is now on Manners Mall. They would sit quietly together and she would tell him: 'We used to be here – this is our place.'

Hannah's father, Taare Warahi (Charles Wallace), was born at Te Aro Pā in 1848.[1] He wore many hats. Koro Charles was an assessor for the Native Land Court and he was a 'licensed Native interpreter'. He was a skilful translator, a man trusted by people at the most senior levels in Māori and Pākehā society. In 1879, for example, Koro Charles was allowed to bring *Lyttelton Times* journalist Samuel Croumbie-Brown on to Parihaka. In front of forty of his more senior male and female Taranaki relatives, Koro Charles translated and interpreted an epic six-hour conversation between the journalist and Te Whiti. Tohu was there but he did not speak. Koro's tact and quick wit, not to mention his extraordinary way with words in English and Māori, kept the kōrero flowing.[2]

Hannah's uncles were living at Parihaka when the pā was invaded. Mohi Parai stayed there afterwards. He was among the dozens of Taranaki men who were arrested for non-violent protests between 1897 and 1898.[3] It is likely that Hannah's aunty (Turia Warahi – Julia Wallace) was there too. Hannah's house was on Fraser Avenue, Johnsonville. Fraser Avenue intersects with Haumia Street, named for the Taranaki hapū of Hannah's grandmother Arapera Rongouaroa Parai and her great-grandfather Hemi Parai. Arapera died in Wellington in 1883. We have one photograph. It's been coloured by hand. Her korowai has been tinted a soft brown. She has a blue high-collared blouse underneath, and she wears a raukura in her hair. The white feather, a symbol of followers of Te Whiti, has been painted on after the fact. Don't forget, whānau! Matai Parai, the nephew of Mohi and the son of Parihaka ploughman Te Awhe, was the last one of us to farm our ancestral land at Orimupiko, before the land passed into the hands of a Pākehā family, our 'tenants' for more than seventy years.[4]

Now you know who I am.

In 2001, when I first met Parihaka leader, artist and historian Te Miringa Hōhaia to discuss the PhD I wanted to write, he took us back to Te Aro as well. He mentioned Paua, a bar that used to be in the Oaks complex. He liked going there when he was in town. 'It's our place,' he said. 'We belong there.'

In 2012 I was looking at a block order file in the Māori Land Court office in Whanganui, and saw Hōhaias next to Warahis (Wallaces) and Parais on the same piece of nineteenth-century paper related to land at Orimupiko, Ōpunake. All those old people stepped towards me, shutting down the distance between Taranaki and Wellington, past and present. Te Miringa had passed away in mid 2010, so I couldn't say to him: 'Now I know what you meant! Now I get it!' It's sad to consider how many people have died before the claims they devoted so much of their lives to have been resolved.

History is a discipline that separates the present from the past. The historian climbs to the summit of a mountain made not of rock but of paper. For seventeen years she piles up books and scholarly articles and photocopies of archival papers, then she stands on that summit and surveys, condenses and explains. She attempts a timeline of cause and effect. First there was this and then there was that and then the next thing. The past has to begin and end somewhere, though, and that is the first problem. Where did Parihaka come? The historian descends the paper mountain. She starts to poke about in several ravines, searching for an answer and an easy, accessible way to foreground the history of Parihaka for a general reader. Then the daughter of the translator speaks and the paper rustles and flies off. 'We used to be here – this is our place.'

KING TIDES

Te Whiti and Tohu, the young men who would one day lead Parihaka, left Taranaki during the wars before the wars, and were living at Waikanae. There they met Minarapa, the man who ministered to my ancestors at Te Aro Pā in what is now central Wellington. Minarapa baptised them. In 1840 Minarapa went back to Taranaki, and Tohu and Te Whiti were among those who accompanied him. It was the start of a great return migration.[5]

People returned to their ancestral homes in Taranaki as increasing numbers of New Zealand Company settlers arrived in the place that was now called Port Nicholson. Natural disasters sped the return migration. In 1848 Te Aro Pā and the other settlements around the harbour shook for three days, draining Te Aro swamp and destroying Waitangi stream – both important sources of food and water. Another big quake in 1855 caused further damage.

The Taranaki some of my people returned to was greatly changed. At Ngā Motu, there was a place called New Plymouth. New Zealand Company ships had been and gone, leaving more British people behind. Parliament created the province of Taranaki in 1853. 'The king tides carried waves of settlers, eroding the earth, consuming the land, deep concern builds,' as the English translation of Parihaka's legacy statement says of the period between 1840 and 1860.[6] Christian orators flourished. Minarapa built a church at his pā at Rāhotu and preached all along the coast, while Johann Friedrich Riemenschneider, a Lutheran, set up a mission school at Wārea in 1846. Te Whiti and Tohu both willingly attended the school, and helped construct and run the flour mill there.

By 1858 there were two-and-a-half thousand English settlers in New Plymouth, and British Army troops and their families in the garrison at Marsland Hill. New Plymouth, like Wellington, was a military settlement and the law there was of the martial variety. Although most people in New Plymouth today do not generally think of the place as a war zone, the sound of te piukara (the bugle in a military brass band) can still be heard in the names of walkways like Red Coat Lane, which runs along Huatoki stream, linking Marsland Hill – the site of the nineteenth-century military barracks – with lower Carrington Street, where the British soldiers used to train.

The pressure on Māori land was acute, and Taranaki leaders formed a league that swore no more land would be sold. But some decided to go their own way and sell to settlers. In March 1860 surveyors entered land at Waitara that had been 'sold', and Te Ātiawa leader Wiremu Kīngi Te Rangitāke turned them away. On 17 March 1860 war began at Waitara between soldiers of the British Army and Te Ātiawa people and their allies. Two weeks after that, the British naval ship the *Niger* bombed the pā next to the Wārea mission. The assault went on for two days and two nights. The coast there is carpeted in black stones and boulders, and after the bombing the pā was carpeted in cannonballs. Five hundred soldiers and sailors marched down from New Plymouth to finish the warship's work. They demolished the mill, burnt stacks of harvested wheat, tore up crops and ransacked pā. In 2012 I went on a Taranaki hīkoi that visited this place, and perhaps it was not just my imagination that made it seem so bleak. Niger is still the name of one of the dorms at New Plymouth Boys' High School.

In June 1860, after Te Ātiawa and their allies defeated the British Army at the Battle of Puketakauere, close to Waitara, European settlers dug an entrenchment to ring the entire inner settlement from Mt Eliot (Puke Ariki) up Queen and Robe streets to the military barracks at Marsland Hill, and then around to the corner of Liardet and Courtenay streets and all the way back down to the beach. Eight blockhouses formed a further ring of defence a little further out. As archaeologist Nigel Prickett has noted: 'New Plymouth was the only settler town to be enclosed in a continuous work, although Wellington, Wanganui and Auckland all had blockhouse defences at different times in the wars.'[7]

Pākehā women and children were evacuated to Nelson. Māori fought with ammunition taken from imperial soldiers or, more often, crude bullets they made themselves from nails, tea-chest lead, newspaper or pages of the Bible.[8] Even with homemade bullets, we managed to do our share of the killing. Everyone was afraid. This was a war. William Strutt's controversial 1861 painting, 'View of Mt Egmont, Taranaki, New Zealand, taken from New Plymouth, with Maoris driving off settlers' cattle', imagines a scene from one side of this war.[9] In the 1860s Māori people did not have the time or money to produce our own paintings or sketches or even a quick carving, because we were fighting to survive. So, the visual record of the wars is completely skewed.

People returning home, people fleeing homes, people arriving to set up new homes, a sentry on every street corner, warriors hidden in pits: Taranaki was in chaos. Nothing was clear. Nothing was stable. Identities and allegiances shifted quickly. Tikanga was remade overnight. No shame in being a turncoat. A turncoat might survive. A Christian God, a Māori God, a Māori King, a British Queen, an English language, te reo Taranaki. Where to settle? How to settle? How to read this world of fire and upheaval? Fight? Flee? Hide? Pray? Be totally and utterly passive. Do it all.

Wounded lay on pews, churches became hospitals. In September 1862 in Ōpunake, a Royal Mail vessel, the *Lord Worsley*, was wrecked at Namu Bay, and Wiremu Kīngi Te Matakātea and his people helped sixty-six passengers ashore. As the historical account in the Taranaki iwi deed of settlement puts it, at the time the boat went aground Māori at Ōpunake were threatening to kill any Pākehā who entered the area without permission.

For Taranaki prophet Te Ua Haumēne, the arrival of the *Lord Worsley* sparked a 'personal crisis arising from the incompatibility of this approach and his own Christian beliefs'. Kapariera (the Angel Gabriel) visited him and told him to 'cast off the yoke of Pākehā domination'.[10] Te Ua (the backbone, the resolute) shed his baptismal name – Horopāpera Tūwhakararo, a transliteration of John Zerubbabel – for his new title. Te Ua developed the Paimārire faith and it spread quickly through Taranaki, up the Whanganui River, and into the Bay of Plenty and Waikato. Te Ua baptised and named the Māori King, Tāwhiao.

Puke Ariki, the museum and library in New Plymouth, has a small physical remnant of Te Ua's faith – a band from a niu pole. Followers would hoist three or more flags to the top of a pole: one for peace (Ruru), one for war (Riki) and one for the leader who conducted the ceremony. They believed the Paimārire rituals would make them bulletproof. When I saw the rusted band, and handled it, I felt nothing, though the name attached to it on the museum's database was familiar from a whakapapa chart. The rusted metal held no magic. Its power remains at Whakamāra, the pā in south Taranaki that the Armed Constabulary destroyed in 1869 as they chased another Taranaki leader, Tītokowaru. The Puke Ariki catalogue says the niu pole this band came from was eighty feet high, made from solid rimu, '4 or 5 feet through at the butt'.[11]

Some Taranaki people still use the words 'Paimārire' (good and peaceful) as a greeting or farewell. I've heard it at Parihaka and I've heard it on Pōmare Day at Ōwae Marae in Waitara. One of

Te Ua's young followers was Te Kāhui Kararehe, the son of Minarapa Te Rangihautuake – the man who built the first church in Wellington at Te Aro and who also baptised Te Whiti and Tohu. Te Miringa Hōhaia relates that when Te Kāhui was only fourteen, he fought with Te Ua's tāua. He went on to become a scribe at Parihaka in the 1870s, and his writings have been a primary source for the work of Taranaki historians like Te Miringa Hōhaia and Ruka Alan Broughton before him. Te Kāhui's manuscripts are a primary source for Hēmi Sundgren's work as a co-author (with Office of Treaty Settlements historian John Armstrong) of the compelling historical account in the 2014 Taranaki iwi deed of settlement. The manuscripts also fed into Parihaka's He Puanga Haeata legacy statement, written by Ruakere Hond and Sundgren.

Paimārire, Te Ua, young Te Kāhui's education: they all started in little old Ōpunake. People wear their pyjamas to the fish and chip shop there. I stayed at the caravan park next to Ōpunake beach with my children at the start of 2013. We had driven up from Wellington for a hui about Orimupiko. When we arrived, the beach was packed. It was like nothing had ever happened there except for Mr Whippy and sunshine. At night, two pierced backpackers from Holland snuck into the camp kitchen from their humpy outside the caravan-park fence. I saw them later through the hedge, two outlines spinning fire sticks in the dark. They were freeloaders but I liked them anyway. It was beautiful to watch their lean bodies move, so light and quick, and to hear the whoosh of the flaming sticks as they drew their pictures in the air.

Up above the beach and the campground there's a small urupā, a scrap that escaped alienation. My whanaunga, the poet J.C. (Jacquie) Sturm, is buried there. The poet James K. Baxter was married to her. 'Tricky Business', a history poem Sturm wrote for the *Parihaka: The Art of Passive Resistance* exhibition, describes the situation for our relatives after the invasion of Parihaka.

Can you see –
Smoke from burning whare
Darkens the face of the sun
Maunga Taranaki
Covers his head with cloud[12]

Sturm's words also refer back to the military campaigns of the second Taranaki war (1863–66). Pākehā called the followers of Te Ua the Hau Hau. Te Ua preached peace but many of his followers acted violently, killing missionaries and attacking (and sometimes beheading) British soldiers. The retribution for these acts was brutal. Māori did not have enough to eat and they did not have anywhere safe to sleep because the imperial troops and their allies began to destroy their farms and burn their homes. The British introduced 'bush scouring', as military historians call it, in north Taranaki in 1863. In four days in April 1864, colonial and imperial troops and Māori who were fighting with the Crown destroyed 'every cultivation within 20 miles south of New Plymouth', decimating Taranaki iwi kāinga.[13] In 1865 and 1866, General Trevor Chute led scorched-earth campaigns through south Taranaki. In six weeks in early 1866, General Chute and his men destroyed seven pā and twenty kāinga in the area.

The refugees of war who had returned to Taranaki from Wellington and Waikanae were made refugees many times over in their homes around the mountain. After Wārea was bombed, Te Whiti and Tohu retreated with Ngāti Moeahu and Patukai to land at Ngākumikumi. General Chute destroyed that settlement in 1865, and the two leaders moved to Waikoukou. Soldiers burnt that as well a few months later. Finally, in 1866, Te Whiti and Tohu and their followers moved further inland to a remote village in the bush west of Taranaki maunga – Parihaka, in the centre of Taranaki iwi rohe.

ASHES TO ASHES
The world around them was ash. Dozens of kāinga along the coast had been destroyed. Hunger was the only harvest. Legislation was a fuse for further

fires, ones that still burn today in perpetual leases or other tortuous ownership mechanisms for the fragments of Māori land that remain in Taranaki – land that is marooned in an ocean of West Coast Lease land that has been 'converted' to freehold and is farmed by other people. The Māori owners of the scraps of land that are left may no longer know each other at all. Half of them may live in Australia or even further afield. Some will be dead. No one has sorted out succession because the fourteen-page form from the Māori Land Court is cumbersome – and if the owner of the land died without a will, forget it!

The enraged colonial government wanted to be emphatic. How dare these people keep fighting back? How dare they insist? It was not enough to merely burn Taranaki people's homes and uproot their crops – houses could be rebuilt, gardens replanted, marae remade – the government had to remove the land on which these lives were built. It used paper to burn the land itself. The New Zealand Settlements Act 1863 turned Taranaki to ash.

The Act and other confiscation legislation are reproduced in full as an appendix to the Waitangi Tribunal's Taranaki Report (1996). The word confiscate makes me think of the small punishments we used to inflict on our children. The toys we would confiscate, the TV time. Later, the mobile phones. It is a sign of power to be in the position even to suggest confiscation, let alone enact it.

Whereas the Northern Island of the Colony of New Zealand has from time to time been subject to insurrections amongst the evil-disposed persons of the Native race to the great injury, alarm and intimidation of Her Majesty's peaceable subjects of both races and involving great losses of life and expenditure of money in their suppression And Whereas many outrages upon lives and property have recently been committed and such outrages are still threatened and of almost daily occurrence And Whereas a large number of inhabitants of several districts of the Colony have entered into combinations and taken up arms with the object of attempting the extermination or expulsion of the European settlers and are now engaged in open rebellion against Her Majesty's authority ...[14]

How quickly Her Majesty and Her Majesty's men assumed authority and how extensive that authority was. The Crown had more men, and these men had all the food, weapons and clothes they needed. As historian Charlotte Macdonald's Soldiers of Empire project has revealed, at the peak of the wars, twelve thousand British soldiers were sent to New Zealand to fight against Māori in Waikato, Tauranga and Taranaki. They came from Sydney and the goldfields in Victoria. Several regiments even came from India. Guns and men, cannons and warships, military bands and rum and, best of all, the promise of a piece of land for each soldier at the end of it. The soldiers would become farmers.

The New Zealand Settlements Act, the government said, would allow for 'the permanent protection and security of well-disposed inhabitants of both races'. Congenial members of each race would be protected by 'the introduction of a sufficient number of settlers able to protect themselves and to preserve the peace of the Country'.[15] The Taranaki iwi deed of settlement records that the British Colonial Office was wary of the Act and warned the Governor, George Grey, to apply it in a just and modest fashion, and to protect 'the lands of innocent people and tribes'. In mid 1865, the Governor used the Act to confiscate all of what it called 'middle Taranaki' – the entire Taranaki iwi rohe, 560,000 acres. By the end of the year, the Governor had massively extended the confiscation area to the north and south-east, into Ngāti Ruanui and Te Ātiawa rohe. Another 854,000 acres was declared confiscated.

The land was tugged out from under Taranaki feet. Even the mountain was taken.

With everything gone, the Crown still was not satisfied. In April 1865 it sent an agent to Ōpunake and insisted that two Taranaki iwi leaders, Wiremu Kīngi Te Matakātea and Arama Karaka Te Raeuaua, swear allegiance to the Crown. The men did so because Te Ua, the founder of Paimārire, had declared fighting should cease. He too had to swear allegiance to the Crown. The Taranaki iwi deed of settlement includes a fragment from a speech Te Raeuaua gave at the time of the Taranaki 'surrender'. He used rape as a metaphor for the Crown's forcible taking of land and resources.[16]

By 1865, Te Ua was unwell but 'two new leaders were consecrated to continue his work. For the next forty years, Tohu Kākahi and Te Whiti o Rongomai led Māori from Taranaki and elsewhere in a campaign characterised by acts of non-violent resistance to bring an end to conflict and confiscation in Taranaki.'[17]

Paimārire had another influential disciple as well: Ngāti Ruanui rangatira Riwha Tītokowaru, a baptised Methodist like Te Whiti and Tohu. Two significant historians, Hōhaia and James Belich, have emphasised the importance of Tītokowaru in the development of non-violent resistance.[18]

In his book *I Shall Not Die* and in *The Dictionary of New Zealand Biography*, James Belich argues Tītokowaru had been a Christian pacifist in 1850, then became a Māori nationalist in 1860 when he took part in raids near New Plymouth. In 1864 he lost his right eye in the failed attack on Te Mōrere (Sentry Hill). It was Te Ua, as Belich puts it, 'who brought about Titokowaru's second conversion to peace'. In late 1866, Tītokowaru rebuilt Te Ngutu-o-te-manu, a large marae in south Taranaki. He declared 1867 to be 'the year of the daughters, the year of the lamb'. He hosted large peace hui at his rebuilt marae and led peace hīkoi around Taranaki. 'Often wrongly portrayed as having been a cover for preparation for conflict, Titokowaru's Peace was in fact as remarkable, and unsung, an achievement as Titokowaru's War,' Belich writes.[19]

Taranaki's third war, Tītokowaru's war, began in 1868 when he ordered his men to kill soldier-settlers on confiscated tribal land at Pātea. He was an outstanding military tactician, and within six months Tītokowaru and his hundreds of followers had expelled all colonial soldiers in south Taranaki; but he withdrew from a fortified pā, Tauranga Ika, as the colonists were about to attack again. He hid 'up the back of Taranaki' in Ngāti Maru.

The third conversion to peace was in the 1870s when Tītokowaru formed an alliance with Parihaka, a move that greatly enhanced the mana of Te Whiti and Tohu.

Te Whiti declared 'the lion shall lie down with the lamb'. Artist Marion Maguire's lithograph, 'Te Whiti and Titokowaru discussing the question "what is peace?"', is a beautiful reminder of the sorts of profound questions these two leaders were asking themselves and their followers back then.

In 1878 Tītokowaru's followers turned back surveyors who entered his cultivations at Taikatu Pā, south of Parihaka. The surveyors cut lines through cultivations, burial grounds and grass-seed crops that Tītokowaru was selling to white settlers. Ngāti Ruanui people pulled up survey pegs and chopped them up for kindling. Tītokowaru was also arrested for 'obstructing Charles Wilson Hursthouse [a surveyor and road engineer] an authorised person under the West Coast Settlements Act 1880' during the invasion of Parihaka.[20] He was put in solitary confinement at Pungarehu and went on a hunger strike that ended only when constables prepared to force-feed him with a tube. Tītokowaru was an old man by then, well into his sixties, and weak with asthma, heart disease and rheumatism. He died seven years after te pāhua, and two thousand people attended his tangi.

Although Tītokowaru is far from a household name in Pākehā New Zealand he is recalled in Taranaki Māori families, even the ones who are living in Australia. In 2011, I was looking at Lily's school photo and noticed that one of her classmates had a striking first name: Tītokowaru. This gave me pause. Then I realised that one half of the boy's double-barrelled surname was familiar too: Anderson. I knew that name. Blair Anderson. Auntie Betty Anderson. Pātea. Wallaces. Māori Land Court in Whanganui.

'Guess what, Lil? You know that boy T? He's your cousin!'

'So?'

I was walking the dog a couple of weeks later when I heard a voice shouting over the railway tracks. It was Jimmy, the toughest kid at Altona Primary. He was with T. 'Hey, T says you're his aunty. That true?'

NEW WEAPONS

Parihaka welcomed not just members of the Taranaki iwi but any Māori person who was prepared to follow the kaupapa of non-violent protest. While the non-violence was a spiritual, political stance, it was also pragmatic. By 1866, Māori were radically outnumbered by well-armed soldiers and settlers. The British Army was preparing to leave the colony but the local Armed Constabulary and volunteer militia forces took over. New weapons were needed – weapons disguised in gestures, symbols, buildings, words and actions.

'What separated Parihaka from other forms of resistance used by rangatira such as Titokowaru, Te Rangitaake, and Te Ua Haumēne was not any underlying difference in objective or ideology but simply a difference in method or strategy,' writes Ruakere Hond. 'Tohu and Te Whiti adopted alternative approaches to the traditional response to conflict. They were able to break with tradition in order to respond to their circumstances.'[21]

The Crown declared Taranaki land confiscated

in 1865 but it did not send 'settlers' (that is, non-Māori people who were born overseas) to occupy confiscated land right away. Fighting continued in Taranaki, then it stopped, then it started again with Tītokowaru's attack on soldiers in Pātea in 1868. By 1869 Tītokowaru had withdrawn, and the Crown was busy with Te Kooti's war in the East Coast, Taupō, Tongariro and Te Urewera. In Taranaki, there was a lull. The king tide receded. Māori built tollgates along the old beach road by the coast. My relatives said who could come and who could go, and they charged people for the privilege. The understanding was that no land in the Taranaki iwi rohe – roughly from Ōkato in the north to the Waingongoro River just south of Manaia – would be made available for settlers until the Crown had provided reserves for locals, including the hundreds of people who now lived at Parihaka.[22]

But land was not set aside, and in 1878 surveyors entered Tītokowaru's territory south of Parihaka to begin surveying the Waimate Plains prior to sale. Te Whiti's requests for information about the promised reserves came to nothing. In May 1879 he sent out the first team of men to plough Māori land that had been occupied by 'settlers'. Between 30 June and 31 July 1879, 182 men and boys were arrested for ploughing, charged and sent to Mt Cook barracks in Wellington pending their shipment to jails in Lyttelton or Dunedin. Laws were introduced that allowed most prisoners to be held without trial.[23]

In July 1879 Land Purchase Commissioner William Williams was one of those who spoke at a hearing for eleven Parihaka ploughmen who had been arrested for ploughing 'Mr John Finlayson's land at Normanby' and planting potatoes on it. Williams told the Resident Magistrates Court in Pātea that the men 'knew they were breaking the law, and that they were doing it not merely to plough up the land, but to plough up the feelings of the government'.[24]

Koro Charles Wallace was the interpreter in court that day, and he has left us the following translation of an exchange between a man the newspaper calls 'Tuki Tuki' (Tukino) and Farquar Finlayson, a farmer at Manaia:

Tuki Tuki – Who does the land belong to?

Mr Finlayson – The land belongs to John Finlayson, my brother.

Tuki – Who gave the land to John Finlayson?

Mr Finlayson – My brother holds the Crown grant for it.

Tuki – Who sold you that land?

My Finlayson – The land was purchased from a man named Allen.

Tuki – Who did Allen buy it from?

Mr Finlayson – Allen obtained it from a man named Moeller.

Tuki – Who did Moeller buy it from?

Mr Finlayson – He bought it from some of the Wanganui Native Contingent to whom it was granted by ... Government for their services.

Tuki – Who gave the land to the Government?[25]

The dialogue ended before Finlayson could answer. 'The court declined to allow the discussion to go any further, as the action was not a question of title,' the newspaper report said. I laughed when I read that line. The action was precisely a question of title. That was the only point Tukino was making.

Two months later, Koro Charles was fortunate to be allowed to enter Parihaka and to listen to Te Whiti speak about politics, and then to translate Te Whiti's views into English. Koro Charles was with *Lyttelton Times* journalist Croumbie-Brown. The latter wanted to know 'about the Native difficulty'. Koro Charles told him that Te Whiti said the land had been wrongly confiscated. It had to be returned to Māori and it would be returned, via the (ploughmen) prisoners who had 'allowed themselves to be arrested'.[26]

In a separate report, Koro Charles worked with Croumbie-Brown to dramatise key moments in the long dialogue with Te Whiti and render them as direct speech.

Te Whiti: I do not know whether it is of any use my tiring out my lips to tell you about the way in which the Government has wronged us. What I mean by wronging us is this – thieving our land, and then calling it 'confiscation' (rau o te patu). Did you not hear, in the South Island, about the land that was taken from us, and then called 'confiscated land'?

Myself [Croumbie-Brown]: Yes, we have heard all about what the Government call 'confiscated land'...

Te Whiti: I do not think the people have any power over the Government; the Government rule the people. We do not complain of the people, but of the Government. I am quite sure that if the people had the power we would have justice done.[27]

Historian Hazel Riseborough rightly points out that Pākehā translators of Te Whiti's speeches, such as R.S. Thompson, used conjecture and inference to express ambiguous statements, but in the words chosen by Koro Charles I see a delicate touch that conveys, even now, at least some of the power contained in the words uttered by Te Whiti and his followers. Riseborough also notes that Croumbie-Brown was something of an opportunist (is there a journalist who is not?) and he initially went to Parihaka as both a correspondent and a government spy. It did not take long, though, for Croumbie-Brown to switch his allegiances, and he was soon producing influential anti-government, pro-Parihaka reports for the *Lyttelton Times*.[28] Again, I believe the skill of Koro Charles had some influence on this shift.

In late 1879 the government passed the Confiscated Lands Inquiry and Maori Prisoners Trials Act, and the resulting West Coast Commission into the 'alleged grievances' of Parihaka people held its first hearing in February 1880.

The West Coast Commission never sat at Parihaka and it took evidence only from Māori people who were 'loyal' to the Crown.[29] Even so, it recommended that the government stop plans for surveys or roads until proper reserves had been granted along the West Coast.

In 1880, when Parliament passed an updated version of the Maori Prisoners Trials Act – the legislation suspended the ordinary course of law and allowed prisoners to be imprisoned without trial indefinitely – the member for Eastern Māori, Hawke's Bay politician Hēnare Tomoana, was one of those who spoke up against it. He said, 'Te Whiti has always said he cares not to fight. His only weapon is his tongue … he has no firearms, no gunpowder. His tongue and his voice are all he uses.'[30]

Meantime, despite the commission's recommendations, Native Minister John Bryce ordered six hundred heavily armed men disguised as 'road builders' to move into the Waimate Plains. In my thesis and book, I have analysed the way the government hid its desire to crush the last bastion of independent Māori power in Taranaki behind the construction of infrastructure. A road, a telegraph line, a lighthouse – these were merely necessary components of modernity. Why were the people of Parihaka so backward?

Te Whiti sent out boys and men to repair fences that had been torn down by soldier-road builders and, in some cases, to put up fences across the unwanted road that was under construction. Surveyor Stuart Newall's hand-drawn maps are compelling evidence that the road builders were purposefully cutting through Parihaka cultivations. Between 19 July and 5 September 1880, 223 boys and men were arrested for fencing and sent to jails in Lyttelton and Dunedin.

The tortuous wording of the charges against the Parihaka men demonstrates just how hard the Crown had to work in Taranaki to impose its definitions and its laws on the land. Here is what a member of the Armed Constabulary wrote next to the names of about a dozen men arrested for fencing:

That they did at a certain place to whit Pungarehu in the County of Taranaki in the Colony of New Zealand within the confiscated territory mentioned in the West Coast Settlement Act 1880 wilfully and unlawfully place upon a certain Road such Road being a highway which The Governor by notice in the Gazette has declared to be a highway in accordance with the provision of said Act a certain obstruction to wit pieces of fencing with a view of impeding the free use of such highway on the part of Her Majesty's subjects on the 4th day of September 1880.[31]

You really can't make this stuff up. You say the

sky is blue, I say it is green. If one side will not accept the truth of the other, then you can turn your opponents' world upside down, and that is what the Crown did in Taranaki. It arrested and imprisoned most of the men, and left the women and children with the task of growing enough food for a large settlement that attracted hundreds of visitors a month – a task that was complicated by the presence of hundreds of heavily armed men.

In 1881 the government decided to survey land for sale on the block between Parihaka and the sea, a site of ancestral cultivations. At the same time the political prisoners were released from jail in Dunedin, Hokitika and Lyttelton, and allowed to return to Parihaka. As ships docked at Ōpunake with more 'dangerous' returned prisoners, the government sent even more troops to Taranaki. An ultimatum was issued. Accept the reserves, the 'large and ample reserves', that were promised; accept the authority of the Queen, or … lose the lot. The answer Parihaka gave was to sit down quietly and wait. On 5 November 1881 the invasion force entered the pā. There was one soldier for every two residents, extra garrisons of men at Pungarehu and Rāhotu, an Armstrong cannon up on the hill. The children skipped and sang, the women carried bread they had baked for the troops. The Riot Act was read, obviously. You say the sky is blue. I say it is green.

3. THE VERY LONG SORRY

Between 1991 and 2018 the New Zealand government has apologised nine times for the 1881 invasion and ransacking of Parihaka. First, the Crown apologised at Parihaka in 1991 at the start of the sixth hearing of the Waitangi Tribunal's Taranaki inquiry. Then the Crown apologised for invading Parihaka in each settlement it has reached with seven of the eight Taranaki iwi: Ngāti Tama and Ngāti Ruanui (2001); Ngaa Rauru Kiitahi (2003); Ngāti Mutunga (2005); Te Ātiawa and Ngāruahine (2014); and Taranaki iwi (2015). An agreement in principle with the one other Taranaki iwi, Ngāti Maru, was reached in December 2017, and it is likely this settlement will also mention Parihaka in the apology. The most prominent apology was Te Puanga Haeata (the new dawn or new year), the one the Crown delivered at Parihaka in June 2017.

The New Zealand Police has also expressed remorse. Its forerunner, the New Zealand Constabulary Force, supplied 644 of the men who invaded Parihaka, not to mention supplying all the men who arrested ploughmen and fencers. As the one hundredth anniversary of the invasion approached in 1981, some Parihaka people decided to initiate reconciliation with the police.[1] The Commandant of the New Zealand Police College, Superintendent Maurie Cummings, said 'it would be fitting for the police to respond positively' and he arranged for a small party to attend the commemoration. Sergeant Basil Johnson, a fluent Māori speaker, and Police Museum curator Senior Constable Barry Thomson were instructed to liaise with Constable Norrie Keenan, who was 'well connected with the Parihaka community'. With the cooperation of the Commissioner of Police, the party gained a high-level leader, Inspector Sherwood Young.

Archbishop Paul Reeves was among those who welcomed the delegation on to Parihaka and he invited the police to speak. Historian Richard Hill recalls that after brief opening words from Inspector Young, the police spoke via Basil Johnson. 'There is no known record of what Sergeant Johnson said that day, but essentially it was within the reconciliatory parameters established by the Commandant ... At the very least an apology was implicit in the words spoken by Messrs Young and Johnson, and the latter's speech may have made it explicit.' Informal discussions afterwards indicated that tangata whenua present had accepted the reconciliatory words of the Police speakers as sincere and meaningful, Hill recalls.[2]

As well as the official Crown apologies and conciliatory remorse of the New Zealand Police delegation, Parihaka has given rise to a surfeit of unofficial apologies. In 2010 people who attended the Parihaka Peace Festival could buy black and red 'Arohamai remember Parihaka' apology T-shirts, and so express their individual sorrow and regret.[3] Poets, painters, playwrights, photographers, composers, curators, historians and novelists have paid homage to Parihaka by producing work that urges people to remember what happened there and to reflect on its meanings in the present. Even by the standards of a well-documented 'age of apology', Parihaka has attracted an over-abundance of remorse and regret. It's like a meme. The sorry meme has two parts. The first part is the apology for the historical injustice, and the second part is the apology for forgetting the historical injustice. Sorry about that. Never forget. Sorry about that. Never forget. Sorry about that …

But these things don't stick. Even some of the apologies have been forgotten!

Until very recently, Crown apologies appear to

have magnified rather than mitigated grievance at Parihaka. They have done little to aid either local or national remembrance and understandings of what Parihaka is all about, and what the Taranaki wars meant and continue to mean for Taranaki Māori. Why might that be? The answer is not to do with the sincerity of the Crown's apologetic utterances or the dedication and skill of the many Māori and Pākehā people involved in the Waitangi Tribunal and settlement processes. Rather, the problem lies in common misunderstandings of wrongdoing and its aftermath, especially the sort of sustained wrongdoing that was committed in the nineteenth century as an already weakened Taranaki was forcibly occupied and settled by people from Britain and by settler farmers and soldiers from the Australian colonies. Serious wrongdoing and loss generate an enormous amount of shame, anger and sorrow that flows down through generations. But how is this shame distributed? Who feels it most? How can it best be banished or, at least, offset somehow?

This chapter discusses the place of the apology in Treaty settlements and summarises the Crown apologies. The next chapter, 'Beating shame', changes perspective to discuss the ways in which Taranaki people have worked to flip the script and turn around the pain of historical events by acts of determined, creative and provocative remembrance. I discuss how this local, intimate, whānau-centred work provides some exciting possibilities for new kinds of historical scholarship but it also illuminates a significant problem with Crown apologies. Namely, there is a disconnect between what the Crown says about the past, supposedly on behalf of the nation, and what non-Māori people say about it inside their homes. Until this gap between national history and domestic history is closed, the wars in Taranaki and the invasion of Parihaka will remain events on the margins, or beyond the margins, shadow things, fog happenings, whispers in the corridors of 'the dementia wing of history'.[4]

WE THE PEOPLE WILL CONTINUE

The invasion of Parihaka is sometimes described as the final act in the New Zealand wars, and Taranaki itself suffered from the longest 'regional conflict' of these wars. As outlined in Chapter 2, the fighting went from 1860 to 1881, with smaller skirmishes and unrest on either side of these dates. In Taranaki, war encompassed violent exchange, non-violent resistance and what Richard Hill has described in his work on the Armed Constabulary as periods of 'coercive occupation' that were necessary in a 'post-conquest situation'.[5] Given this, it is difficult to imagine a Taranaki Māori agreeing with the sentence that opens Roberto Rabel's essay on

'New Zealand's Wars' in *The New Oxford History of New Zealand*: 'War has generally touched lightly on New Zealand.'[6] There was little that was light about the nineteenth century for people in Taranaki; and the wounds of war, occupation and invasion were intensified by raupatu (confiscation) and the perpetual leasing regime that continues to this day.[7] Our whānau still 'owns' land granted in 1883 by the West Coast Settlement (North Island) Act 1880; it is a perpetual war memorial, policed by twenty-one separate pieces of legislation beginning with the New Zealand Settlements Act 1863 (the confiscation legislation) and ending with the Maori Reserved Lands Amendments Act 1997.[8]

Taranaki, our mountain, was confiscated along with everything else in 1863. As Te Miringa Hōhaia put it in his essay for *Te Maunga Taranaki* (2001): 'In 1978, the Government introduced legislation to return Taranaki as long as it was given back immediately to be a national park. This two-minute event took place at Ōwae Marae at Waitara. Amid heavy emotion and mayhem, the Taranaki Māori Trust Board reluctantly yielded to the Government's duress. The mountain was lost to its people.'[9] The Trust Board and iwi lodged claims with the Waitangi Tribunal in 1989 for the return of the mountain. Many Māori people in Taranaki never even visited the maunga, so great was the loss and pain. As historian Dennis Ngāwhare-Pounamu writes in his doctoral thesis on 'travelling mountain' narratives about Taranaki: 'Throughout the long years of confiscation, the maunga has been the silent observer, the only constant in shifting boundaries and sold land blocks. The iwi takes its name from the maunga and the ancestor, yet many have never climbed upon the maunga.'[10]

The depth of injustice inflicted on Taranaki people is, perhaps, one reason why the Waitangi Tribunal made reference, controversially, to 'the holocaust of Taranaki history'.[11]

These are some of the hard facts of Taranaki history but what do we do about them? It is commonplace to assume that shame is felt, most keenly, by those who have done wrong, by the perpetrators rather than the victims. The Crown's initial apologies indicate that this assumption is also correct for Parihaka. A Taranaki waiata, 'Te Whakamā' (the shame or embarrassment), also suggests that shame belongs to the perpetrators. In 1927 Ngāti Mutunga performed this waiata in Wellington before the Commission of Inquiry into Confiscated Lands. The 2004 deed of settlement explains that 'this song is about the embarrassment and shame "tauiwi" (non-Māori) should feel for the terrible things they did to Māori people in the old days'. This is how the waiata begins:

Kāhore hoki e te whakamā e tau to ngaro
ake nei
E mahi tātou ake e te iwi
E whaiwhaia nei e te ao he ao koha rā e
kupu tautoro mua
Whakaaria mai mo tēnei rangi ka tū
Nā Te Atua tonu i whakahau
I kite ai hoki au i ngā tatau rino
Ka hora te akau ki Ngāmotu rā e ki
Whanganui rā hoki ki Pōneke rā ia
Ki te haupūranga o nga ture Kawana kia …

Such is the shame its conclusion will not be
achieved.
We the people will continue
This world inflicts a realm of pain extending far
into the past.
Display it all for the occasion before us
It was God who urged this
I also saw the steel doors
The seafront stretched out to Ngāmotu to
Whanganui and then to Wellington
To where the laws of the Governor are heaped …[12]

Waiata are sophisticated historical sources. As historian Judith Binney has observed, waiata are challenging primary sources to work with, because even when they are written down 'they will still convey an "original" fluidity of metaphor and meaning'.[13]

I found 'Te Whakamā' when I was ready to respond to the hints my ancestors were giving me about the inescapable complexity of the past and of representing stories about the past, and when I also had access to knowledgeable people who decided to teach me a little. As a result, I now believe that it is Māori, not Pākehā, who have been overwhelmingly burdened by shame as a result of invasion, plunder and confiscation. How do apologies figure in all of this? What relevance do they have to Taranaki?

PARIHAKA APOLOGIES
Apologies are central to the negotiated settlements between the Crown and iwi. Along with cultural redress, and commercial and financial redress, 'The Apology' is one of the three building blocks of a settlement package. It has become mandatory. A 2008 Crown Forestry Rental Trust guide for claimants negotiating Treaty settlements explains that while claimants may have mixed views on an apology – some demand one, while others debate its merits – the 'reality is that the Crown insists on making an apology, even if negotiators do not want one'. The Office of Treaty Settlements' so-called red book, 'Healing the Past, Building a Future', explains that The Apology (the capital letters come courtesy of the red book's authors) makes 'very significant steps towards recognising the mana of the claimant group; restoring the honour of the Crown; and

61

rebuilding the relationship between the Crown and the claimant group'. This may be true for some iwi – especially for Tainui, who elicited an apology from Queen Elizabeth herself – but, until 2017, it was not true at Parihaka, where there has been a mismatch between the responses of the givers and the receivers.

While it is likely that the Crown and its agents heard in the first apologies sincere remorse, respect and a desire to rebuild relationships, Māori initially heard something less positive. Some Parihaka kaumātua viewed the apologies with indifference, anger or even disdain. In 2009 I tested these suspicions with Te Miringa Hōhaia, who encouraged me to provide an 'informed perspective'. He did not think the early apologies had fixed anything at Parihaka either (except for grievances, perhaps!). Te Miringa asked me to consider: 'Why was the Crown apologising about Parihaka anyway? Did it imply that Parihaka was being addressed? Where were Parihaka people in all of this? What does it bode for Parihaka when we negotiate? Was it wise of the Government to make Parihaka apologies in the absence of dialogue with us? Indeed, who negotiated with them on the appropriateness, the content, the dignity required?'[14] At the time, those questions were urgent. Te Miringa was one of the mandated Taranaki iwi representatives working hard to ready our iwi for entering into negotiations.

Te Miringa's comments signal the flaws in a model in which an official apology is supposed to be a pathway to healing grievances and making peace, to putting the past behind us. As philosopher Janna Thompson has argued in relation to Australia and elsewhere, one reason for dissatisfaction with apologies is 'that they seem a poor response to the enormity of injustices that were committed. "We took your lands; we stole your children. Sorry about that".'[15] However, Thompson still sees value in an apology and argues that it 'is best understood as an attempt to make up for the past – an act that cannot succeed but which is necessary to perform'. How, then, is it best to perform it, and what might a well-performed apology achieve?

The Apology is supposed to make everyone feel better, not just the Crown. It is supposed to be an exchange between two groups, a 'reconciliatory gesture', a sign of mutual intent, namely 'rebuilding the relationship' that had been shattered by colonial violence and by the less obvious, but no less lethal, bureaucratic violence that followed. The Apology is symbolic. It does not shut down discussion. It should open it up. For example, The Apology should not preclude other, more difficult apologies that may need to be exchanged between members of different iwi. Māori men were members of the force that invaded Parihaka, and Māori fought with the Crown in Taranaki between 1860 and 1869 too.

It is possible to argue that, at Parihaka, a better kind of apology can restore mana (for Māori) and honour (for the Crown), and so rebuild relationships between the two. To do this, it would need to meet the criteria that Janna Thompson has outlined as necessary for a 'genuine political apology'.[16] Namely, the content of the apology and the ceremony surrounding it should be endorsed by the victims and their representatives, and by the people who live in the nation responsible for the wrong; the government should make sure that the victim's suffering is 'embedded in the official history of the nation', and it should demonstrate that it will no longer harm the victims or their descendants.

I endorse these ambitious criteria. However, none of the Parihaka apologies – including He Puanga Haeata – has yet managed to achieve *all* these aims. And it is clear that the story of Parihaka is far from being embedded in the 'official history of the nation'.

Leaving aside the apology implicit in the findings of the 1927 Sim Commission and possibly even in the findings of the 1880s West Coast Commission, the first Crown apology for the invasion of Parihaka was given, without warning, at the first Waitangi Tribunal hearing at Parihaka in 1991. Solicitor Tom Winitana, a Tūhoe man, spoke on behalf of the Minister of Justice Doug Graham, a Pākehā. Winitana said the Crown did not dispute Taranaki claimants' testimony at the 1927 Sim Commission about the sacking of the village, and it did not dispute claimants' version of events now. The Crown would listen respectfully if people chose to talk about the invasion, but said it did not expect 'any one of you to come before this Tribunal and suffer the distress of re-telling those events'. Rather, Winitana concluded, the Crown was ready to enter into direct negotiations with Taranaki iwi to 'discuss any proposal whereby the mana of Parihaka might be restored':

We are the descendants, the inheritors of that unhappy past. It is our duty to give it a proper burial. It is my duty, as one of Her Majesty's Ministers, to apologise to the ancestors of Parihaka and I now do so. In doing so I look now to the future. It beckons us all. Let us stand together as we face what is to come.[17]

Parihaka leaders rejected the apology. It had come without warning, they explained, almost as an afterthought. It was addressed to the dead rather than the living – the descendants of those who had 'lived through the sacking and looting and destruction of Parihaka'. If an apology was to be offered to the living, it would have to be an event of national significance, because Parihaka itself had been a gathering place for iwi from beyond Taranaki. It would have to be offered to a large audience that included Māori from around New Zealand, rather than the smaller group of Taranaki people assembled for a Tribunal hearing. The Parihaka Pā trustees wrote: 'The hurt of Parihaka is therefore felt far beyond Taranaki. What happened there was something of an affront to nations. To the nations which embraced each other as Treaty partners in 1840.'[18] The timing and form of the apology, therefore, would need to be negotiated between the Crown and the people of Parihaka.

The bearer of the apology, the trustees advised, should have a status that matched the status accorded to the invasion of the village, an invasion that 'took place at the direction of the highest authorities'. Even as it was happening, information was being telegraphed directly to both Houses of the General Assembly, they noted. Ideally, an apology should be offered by the Minister of Justice in the presence of the Minister of Māori Affairs and the Prime Minister. Hōhaia and others offered to help the Crown 'along the path' to an apology.

In response, Minister Graham wrote that he was 'deeply disturbed' his apology had been rejected. He had been acting in good faith and believed that his 'personal apology to your ancestors' would demonstrate to Parihaka people that 'as Her Majesty's Minister responsible for Treaty claims I was listening to their grievances with sympathy and understanding'.[19]

Mutual incomprehension and affront char-acterise this exchange. For both sides, the apology damaged rather than enhanced relationships, and eroded the honour of the Crown and the mana of Parihaka. It is interesting to observe that the concerns of the Parihaka Pā trustees anticipate Thompson's arguments about the criteria necessary for a 'genuine political apology'. In their letters, the trustees offer to help the government negotiate an apology that would be appropriately dignified and ceremonial and, therefore, demonstrate the Crown's recognition of Parihaka's mana and the Crown's desire to do no further harm to people who are living there. But the trustees were also letting the government know that any actions taken to make up for the wrong of te pāhua would need to match the actions of the original event. Mahara Okeroa reminded me that the trustees were referring to the fact that utu (payment, satisfaction, a balancing up of accounts) would need to be part of an apology too.

The eight other official apologies have either been negotiated between individual Taranaki iwi and the Crown or, in the case of He Puanga Haeata, between representatives of Parihaka (who whakapapa to many iwi, not just the eight in Taranaki) and the Crown, with the assistance of a high-level working party.

To recap: in 2001, two of the Taranaki tribes, Ngāti Ruanui and Ngāti Tama, signed deeds of settlement with the Crown.[20] In the Ngāti Ruanui deed, the Crown acknowledged 'the serious damage it inflicted on the prosperous village of Parihaka and the people of Ngāti Ruanui residing there', and said its 'treatment of the people of Ngāti Ruanui residing at Parihaka was unconscionable and unjust'. In the Ngāti Tama deed, the Crown made a direct apology 'for its actions at Parihaka'. The 2003 settlement with Ngaa Rauru Kiitahi explained how intimately the south Taranaki iwi was connected with Parihaka and how it suffered greatly as a result of the Crown's actions there. 'The Crown profoundly regrets, and unreservedly apologises to Ngaa Rauru Kiitahi for its actions during the Taranaki wars,' the Apology said. In the 2005 Ngāti Mutunga deed, the Crown again acknowledged the 'serious damage it inflicted on the prosperous village of Parihaka' and its 'unconscionable and unjust' treatment of Ngāti Mutunga people living there. The Apology included the statement: 'The Crown profoundly regrets, and unreservedly apologies for, its unconscionable actions at Parihaka'.

In 2014 the Ngāruahine deed explained that Parihaka was a vital part of the iwi's history and identity. The iwi provided material support to Parihaka, and many of its people were living at Parihaka when it was invaded. The deed said the Crown 'deeply regrets and unreservedly apologises for its unconscionable actions at Parihaka and for the harm those actions caused to the community and to those Ngāruahine people who resided there'. Likewise, the Te Ātiawa deed explains that many Te Ātiawa people participated in Parihaka's campaigns of peaceful resistance. Some received trials but were then detained beyond the period of their sentence, and some died while they were in prison. Te Ātiawa people were also displaced after the invasion of Parihaka. The Crown said it 'profoundly regrets its unjust treatment of those Te Atiawa people it imprisoned for taking part in campaigns of peaceful resistance. The Crown sincerely apologies to those tupuna it exiled hundreds of kilometres from their homes, to the whanau who grieved their absence, to their descendants, and to Te Atiawa.'

Each settlement document acknowledged that the suffering of Māori in Taranaki had been compounded by earlier, botched attempts at making amends. The Ngāti Ruanui deed acknowledged that 'despite previous efforts made in the twentieth century, including those of the Sim Commission, it [the Crown] has failed to deal in an appropriate way with the grievances of Ngāti Ruanui'. Similar statements are contained in all the other deeds.

Peter Adds makes explicit the meanings behind this statement. In his essay for *Contested Ground*, the 2012 book about the Taranaki wars, Adds demonstrates how successive mechanisms that were supposed to fix Taranaki grievances over confiscated land – such as the Sim Commission, the

Taranaki Maori Trust Board (1931), the formation of Parininihi ki Waitotara (1976) and the Waitangi Tribunal hearings (1990–95) – have often multiplied and intensified the problems within and between hapū and iwi, not to mention between Māori and Pākehā. As for Treaty settlements, in Taranaki and elsewhere, Adds argues: 'Bitter public feuds have almost become the norm in this process'.[21]

The Crown has admitted to a poor record in dealing with Taranaki grievances and many Taranaki Māori agree with this assessment. At the Tribunal hearings, claimants were angry about the 'charade' and expense of participating in yet another inquiry when previous ones had failed.[22] In 2000, poet J.C. Sturm despaired at delays in redressing the wrongs of the past, asking: 'How much longer/ must we reap/their bitter harvest?'[23] Given this, it would probably have been wiser for the government to refrain from offering any apology for Parihaka until it had negotiated with representatives of every Taranaki iwi.

There is a model for this approach. No apology has been offered, yet, for the Crown's taking of Taranaki's greatest treasure, Taranaki (Mt Egmont). Instead, each of seven Taranaki settlements already negotiated specifically states that apology and cultural redress in relation to the mountain will be developed in consultation with all iwi. In December 2017 representatives of the eight iwi and the Crown signed Te Anga Pūtakerongo, a record of understanding that will guide negotiations for 'apology and cultural redress' for 'ngā mauuga' – Taranaki, Pouākai and the Kaitake Ranges. Taranaki and the other mountains have been granted legal personhood (like the Whanganui River and Te Urewera), and agreement has been reached that the Mount Egmont Vesting Act (1978) will be repealed, but negotiations on other types of cultural redress and improved governance and custodianship for ngā mauuga are ongoing.[24] Meantime, tramping and skiing clubs and conservation people have more say in the care of Taranaki than iwi do.

Still, there's no point lamenting what might have been in regard to Parihaka. The apologies are out there, and they invert the usual narrative of the victim group who for decades pushes for justice and recognition until, finally, the perpetrator group caves in and utters 'the apology'. Do the Taranaki iwi apology (2015) and the Parihaka one (2017) improve the situation? Are these two most recent apologies better and more enduring that the ones that have come before?

The whakapapa of the most recent apologies gives some room for optimism that we have reached the end of the very long sorry.

Taranaki iwi had been lined up to settle in 2014 at the same time as Te Ātiawa and Ngā Ruahine. Minister for Treaty Negotiations Chris Finlayson was very eager to complete all Taranaki claims during his tenure, but negotiations stalled around Parihaka. Negotiators Mahara Okeroa and Jamie Tuuta walked away from the Taranaki iwi settlement and insisted that the Crown hold separate talks with Parihaka itself. Aside from the three marae at Parihaka – Toroānui, Te Niho o Te Ātiawa and Te Paepae o Te Raukura – there are four other marae within Taranaki iwi's boundaries. The negotiators sought and received a mandate from all seven marae for the strategy of a separate settlement.

In his speech at the first reading of Te Pire Haeata ki Parihaka/The Parihaka Reconciliation Bill on 22 March 2018, Chris Finlayson said he was, and I quote, 'really hacked off' when Taranaki negotiators pulled the pin. In January 2015 Finlayson agreed to set up a working party to advise the Crown on how to support Parihaka towards reconciliation and settlement. Within a few months, Kawe Tuataki (vehicle towards closure), the five-member group chaired by Dame Tariana Turia, had presented the Minister with a hundred-plus-page report, and a reconciliation package was developed – a $9 million development fund, new relationship agreements between Parihaka and local and central government, and legislation that formalises the Crown's commitment to Parihaka. A 'compact of trust' was then signed between Parihaka and the Crown on 22 May 2016.

On 9 June 2017 at Parihaka, Finlayson reminded the audience of that compact. 'When I was here a year ago to sign the compact of trust I spoke about the sense of responsibility I feel as Attorney-General for this reconciliation. The colonial government failed to uphold the rule of law at Parihaka and I am grateful for the opportunity, as the current Attorney-General, to be able to play a part in helping right that past wrong.'[25]

In the speech that preceded the formal Crown apology, Finlayson urged listeners to draw comparisons between the present and the past. 'Today it is almost impossible to imagine any New Zealand government responding to the protests of their citizens by legislating away their right to trial, legalising their continuing detention or retrospectively legitimising the destruction of their homes and possessions,' he said.

'But these things did occur. That is why they must be recorded and remembered … Ultimately, there can be no reconciliation where one party remembers and the other forgets.'

Finlayson also acknowledged the Crown's previous apologies to 'iwi of Taranaki for its many failures to uphold the principles of partnership and good faith that the Treaty of Waitangi embodies, and for the immense harm those actions have caused to generations of Māori in Taranaki.'

At the time of writing, the dual-language

reconciliation Bill was in the select committee phase. In May 2018 the committee went to Parihaka to hear public submissions. On 21 May the *Taranaki Daily News* reported that several speakers asked for a law to 'protect the Parihaka name along with its story' – along the lines of the legal protection granted to Ngāti Toa's 'Ka Mate' haka in 2014. The committee is expected to report back on the Bill in late September. Two more readings will follow, and after Royal Assent has been granted the Bill will become law.

He Kōrero Whakamārama Explanatory Note for the Bill states:

The Crown has apologised for its historical actions at Parihaka in its Treaty of Waitangi settlements with the iwi of Taranaki. However, because of the special place Parihaka occupies in Taranaki and New Zealand, the Crown has committed to reconciling its relationship directly with the Parihaka community. A reconciliation package has been developed for the Parihaka community outside of the Treaty settlement process. The reconciliation package will assist Parihaka to strengthen its infrastructure and achieve other development aspirations.[26]

It is wonderful to see that the commitment to remembering now includes a commitment to remembering previous Crown apologies, even the bungled or half-baked ones. Remembering failure sweetens success.

4. BEATING SHAME

Historian and ethnographer of the Pacific Greg Dening liked to say that all history-making is a dialogue between past and present, and this is a more positive way of describing what other scholars might deride as 'presentism'.

Many Māori, too, seek to point out that the past is often present, here and now, shaping what we do and say and how we think. In one of the last letters he wrote – his 'Heaven Project' letter to Lily and his other mokopuna – Dad touched on the elasticity of time: 'Time of course could be conceived as <u>the ongoing flow of the Now</u> – Always in the Now – despite knowing that there was a yesterday and anticipating tomorrow.' Later in the letter, he paraphrased T.S. Eliot, his favourite poet: 'Time Past and Time Future are both contained within Time Present.'[1]

As I got started on this book, I met with Mahara Okeroa at Raukura, the café in the whare waka on the Wellington waterfront, to go over some ideas. We were discussing te pāhua. He put his thumb and forefinger together. 'I am this close to them,' he said about his mother and grandmother (who was at Parihaka when it was invaded). He got a pen and drew a koru shape on the table. Next to it he drew a straight line. 'That's the distance between me and them,' he said, and pointed at the koru. I was startled and delighted with this gesture. 'You can have that for free!' he said.

Historiographer Berber Bevernage has argued the way we think of historical time strongly influences the way we deal with historical injustice and the ethics of history. Bevernage writes 'that the concepts of time traditionally used by historians are structurally more compatible with the perpetrators' than the victims' point of view, and that breaking with this structural bias demands a fundamental rethinking of the dominant modern notions of history and historical time'.[2]

The past is not an event that can be boxed up, labelled and put away. The past seeps, unfurls, radiates.[3] It is not a straight line but a loop or a coil, a koru. This sense of open-endedness is especially potent for Parihaka, which was a prophetic community. Followers of Te Whiti and Tohu expected the utterances of the two men to shape the future. In 1927, for example, many Māori saw the establishment of the Sim Commission as a fulfillment of Te Whiti's prophecy that peaceful protests would, eventually, force the government to inquire into confiscated lands.[4] In his opening evidence at the first Waitangi Tribunal hearings at Parihaka in 1991, Lindsay Rihari McLeod recited a whakataukī that made a similar point: 'A proverb of Te Whiti is translated as: "The bird startled has flown, only the quiver of the bough remains". We are the quiver – their descendants whom despite all their pain and hurt and feelings of injustice, never taught us to be bitter, vindictive or take revenge.'[5]

An illustration of how the past 'quivers' or reverberates in the present was a photograph on the front page of the *Taranaki Daily News* of 18 March 2010 showing a dignified kuia swinging back a mallet to bang on an enormous red drum. Relatives surrounded the kuia and everyone was dressed in black. Some had albatross feathers in their hair – a symbol of allegiance to the pacifist principles of Te Whiti and Parihaka – and others wore wreaths made from kawakawa leaves. The 'mournful rhythm' of this drum accompanied the opening of the exhibition *Te Ahi Kā Roa, Te Ahi Kātoro Taranaki War 1860–2010: Our Legacy – Our Challenge* at Puke Ariki museum and library in New Plymouth. Later that day at Ōwae Marae in Waitara, the drum beat again as Te Ātiawa leaders,

Prime Minister John Key and Minister of Treaty Negotiations Chris Finlayson signed documents to mark the beginning of settlement negotiations regarding Treaty of Waitangi claims.

Taranaki kaumātua and Anglican Archdeacon Tiki Raumati told a reporter that the drum had been given to his grandmother, who was a leader of poi at Parihaka. 'They used that drum in the military and I will say we turned it around on them and drummed them out with peace and love,' he said.[6] Raumati was reminding newspaper readers that troops played bugles, drums and tin whistles when they marched into Parihaka on 5 November 1881 to invade an unarmed community. We Taranaki people feel terrific pride at the non-violent resistance of Parihaka people, but the plunder has also generated a great deal of shame, remorse, sorrow, anger and suffering for Māori and, to a lesser extent, for Pākehā. The war drum is a fitting metaphor for this shame, which has beaten down through the generations, influencing how we think about ourselves.

For people who have been colonised and their descendants, there are many possible shades of whakamā, from big shames to little ones, from collective 'Māori' shame to specific iwi shame, all the way through to hapū, whānau, and individual, private and personal shame. The varieties of 'big shames' might include shame about the loss of language and land, and about the loss of resources, traditions and leaders. These losses are also serious assaults on mana. Hapū, whānau and individual shames are less obvious, perhaps, but no less damaging to a group's status. They can be about the actions or inactions of your ancestors (including the sale of land, failure to fight, or fighting on the side of the Crown); about the actions or inactions of your living relatives; about the colour of your skin, about your 'blood quantum'; about the place where you live (one of my personal shames – Australia, someone else's tūrangawaewae!); about the absence of korowai or other taonga in your family; about the lack of understanding of what to do at a tangi; about insufficient seafood on the table at a feast, or insufficient speakers on the paepae, or insufficient numbers of women to karanga; or about lack of knowledge of waiata and failure to transmit what knowledge you do have to your children; or even about your own average pronunciation of Māori words – a shame that is perhaps intensified if, like me, you had the privilege of learning from some of the best teachers at an immersion course at the peak of te reo revival in the mid 1980s.

I'm just scratching the surface here. The shame can be internal or it can be external, prompted by relatives or by other Māori people or, of course, by people – relatives, friends and strangers – who are not Māori. The worst shame can be inflicted by your own. In conversation with Alexis Wright, anthropologist Geoffrey Bagshaw referred to the 'closed Aboriginal world, where often the people perceive the enemy as each other, the only people worth getting angry with are your family'.[7]

While Treaty settlements have been a source of pride and astonishing renewal for some iwi – especially Ngāi Tahu – for others they have opened up a whole new realm of shame when settlement money is lost through poor investments or worse. Aboriginal leader Tracker Tilmouth relates a saying from Papunya, in central Australia, that is apt for squandered settlements. *'Big name, no blankets.* You have got a big name but you cannot deliver anything, you cannot produce anything,' Tilmouth told Wright, a novelist who is a member of the Waanyi nation of the Gulf of Carpentaria.[8]

Anthropologist Dame Joan Metge has described whakamā as both a state of mind and a behaviour associated with this feeling. 'Analysis of the situations in which whakamā occurs reveals a variety of causes: shyness, shame not only for wrongdoing but also for being suspected of it, embarrassment over falling short in some respect, feelings of injustice, powerlessness and frustration. The common denominator seems to be "feeling at a disadvantage, being in a lower position morally or socially", whether as a result of your own actions or another's.'[9]

People respond to shame and embarrassment in a number of ways. One common strategy is to forget. Alexis Wright says many families have 'stories that are impossible to resolve. The stories in these families have created a sense of shame or humiliation, and are hidden or destroyed.'[10] Shameful stories are lost through 'deliberate acts of forgetting', through concealment, through not saying anything at all 'because it is not worth the trouble'. Tracker Tilmouth, the subject of Wright's astonishing collective biography *Tracker*, was removed from his family in Alice Springs as a child and sent, with his two younger brothers, to Minjilang (Crocker Island), a mission a thousand kilometres away. Tilmouth talks about the extreme difficulty of finding out where he belonged, the long journey he took to come back, and notes 'a lot of people do not come back. They would rather forget.'[11]

This response, this 'deliberate forgetting', is perfectly articulated in *The Historian Who Lost his Memory*, a short story written by Taranaki leader Te Rangihīroa (Peter Buck) in the early twentieth century and read, much later, by literary scholar Alice Te Punga Somerville in the archives of the Bishop Museum in Honolulu. In this story, the historian narrates ancient tribal events, but when a visitor asks about a 'relatively recent event (a battle at Kaiwhakauka) the historian claims not to know about it'.[12] The rangatira steps in and tells the story, revealing that the historian is the great-grandson of the man who is humiliated in the battle. Then, Te Punga Somerville writes, the visitors 'realise that the historian "lost his memory" because of his own relationship to events'. The historian, in fact, lost his memory because he was ashamed.

Forgetting is rarely innocent. People have to work hard not to know, not to recall, not to see, and to be truly ignorant. Laura Ann Stoler describes ignorance as 'an ongoing operation, a cumulative … and laboured effect' that is achieved and sustained inside 'the social space of family and friendship'.[13] When a family forgets, it is at risk of losing not only the troubling stories but also many other family legacies. Now I can see that one of the things I was doing in my doctoral research and then my book, *The Parihaka Album*, was exploring how shame – about insufficiency, as in a partial or damaged or 'worthless' fraction of Māori-ness, or maybe about excess, a shame about being Māori at all – worked in my family and how this seemingly prevented my grandmother and great-grandmother from passing on valuable information to my father and his cousins and to us, the grandchildren. Damage to whakapapa is one legacy of colonisation. Perhaps it was just easier to forget and become a resident of the dementia wing of history. As Peter Adds has noted, a generation of Taranaki people were taught there was no future in being Māori.[14]

Janna Thompson reminds us that: 'People are caused to suffer not merely by the events themselves but by the ideas they get into their head about these events.'[15] Forgetting is one way of avoiding this suffering, but it comes at a great cost. When possible, a less destructive response to humiliating events is to remember them in a different way, to actively seek to change your relationship to the shameful-painful events, and in so doing to rewrite and repair your history, to try to make something good out of something bad. I owe this insight to tikanga expert Professor Pou Temara, who shared a Ngāti Awa whakataukī on this theme at a symposium on apology at Waikato University in February 2010. The saying is: 'Utua te kino ki te pai – Repay the bad with the good/Whaiho ma te whakamā e patu – Let shame be your punishment.'

In Australia, an example of such radical, creative remembrance is Myall Creek where, in 1838, between ten and twelve white stockmen murdered twenty-eight Wirrayaraay children, women and men in an unprovoked but well-planned attack. It is hard to imagine anything good coming from such an event; yet descendants of both the victims and the perpetrators have tried to turn the event around by working together to erect a monument to the victims of the massacre. The monument was unveiled in 2000 and an annual memorial service is held on the site each year.[16]

The war drum is another example of coping with shame through active, creative, provocative remembering. As Tiki Raumati has observed, Māori claimed a weapon of war, the drum, and 'turned it around on them [the Crown and its allies]', re-presenting it as a weapon for peace.[17] The instruments of the invaders quickly became the instruments of the residents of Parihaka in their own drum and fife bands.[18] A similar 'turning around' is at work in a well-known nineteenth-century waiata, 'Te Piukara' (the bugle), which links the sound of the bugle with the trouble and violence that surrounded Parihaka. The song is chanted like a dirge, yet there is also a triumphant and subtle flick at the end.

The final verse of 'Te Piukara' is: 'Piko mai e kaawana ko ahau to ariki/Ko koe taku pononga e te kuini/kei maunawa', which Te Miringa Hōhaia has translated as: 'Come forth bow down before us Governor I am your lord,/you are my servant/O Queen, source of our oppression./Such trouble.'[19] Here, the victims are claiming a moral victory at the same time as they express suffering.

WHAKAPAPA AND HISTORY

Linda Tuhiwai Smith has written that revisiting history, or 'coming to know the past', is a crucial part of decolonisation, while Dipesh Chakrabarty has urged scholars to think about 'provincializing

Europe' – that is, acknowledging how embedded European understandings are in the ideas that underlie academic history-making.[20] In a similar vein, cultural theorist Stephen Turner has argued that: 'For the settler the Western notion of history is perhaps the deepest form of forgetting a self-constructing form of repression', one that denies 'the experience of contact'.[21]

This 'forgetting' starts close to home, in the family. For instance, one of my Pākehā forebears was John Howard Wallace, a historian and long-time secretary of the Early Colonists Association, whose voluminous papers are held at the Alexander Turnbull Library in Wellington. Wallace spent decades trying to compile a list of early pioneers (those who arrived before 1850) but his feverish work 'forgot' the fact that some of these people, such as his brother William, had married even earlier pioneers – Māori women already living in the places where 'first ships' landed. Wallace Street in Wellington is named after him.

The Treaty claims process creates a community of memory – the Port Nicholson Settlement Block in Wellington, for example – that is based on whakapapa. Every hui, every newsletter, every email re-inscribes the past we share, and reminds us that we are all the product, at some stage, of intimate contact between Māori and Pākehā in either Wellington or Taranaki. The history we are working to turn around is deeply personal as a result. It might be the story of a drum given to a grandmother, or a frightened child singing beneath the haunches of a soldier's horse, or a great-grandfather who drank too much and sold too much land, or a grandmother who declined to use her Māori name.

In the Māori world, I have little standing without whakapapa. In the introduction to a new edition of *Whakapapa*, members of the Māori interest group of the New Zealand Society of Genealogists cite comments made by Dr Pita Sharples during the third reading of the Births, Deaths, Marriages and Relationships Amendment Bill in July 2008. He said:

The Māori Party comes to this Bill driven by the principle of whakapapa. We come to this Bill with a deeply personal understanding of what it means to any discussion of births, deaths marriages and relationships. We, as tangata whenua, hold in the highest regard the value of whakapapa as a means of defining who Māori are as a people. Whakapapa is the bridge that links us to our ancestors, which defines our heritage, gives us the stories which define our place in the world.[22]

Whakapapa works to shape personal identity, but for a person like me, who is also a historian, whakapapa shapes and strengthens research methodologies as well. Building on the groundbreaking work of Linda Tuhiwai Smith, among others, younger Māori scholars have rearticulated the importance of whakapapa and whānau to their research agendas and also sought to extend their work beyond this frame. Arini Loader describes Māori history 'as personal and Māori history is relationships – or put simply, Māori history is whakapapa', but it is also about 'casting the net wider'.[23] Melissa Matutina Williams has considered what stories might be silenced in a Māori-focused research agenda in which researchers want to uphold the mana of their communities and the people they are writing about – although her brilliant book, *Panguru and the City: Kāinga Tahi, Kāinga Rua*, demonstrates that community-centred history can also be complex, subtle and challenging.[24] Nepia Mahuika has also challenged Māori researchers to embrace new theoretical approaches, especially theory and methodologies of oral history-making, and asked whether Māori might look beyond whānau and iwi to 'yet consider producing more of our own bigger and broader histories'.[25] In *Once Were Pacific*, Alice Te Punga Somerville demonstrates what happens when the net is cast wider still to reconnect Māori with our ancestral homelands in the Pacific.[26] In her other work, Somerville examines writing produced by Māori living outside of New Zealand and links this work with international scholarship on indigeneity.

Whakapapa is a web that connects my relatives to a range of local, national and international stories, affirming and destabilising them. History, then, is not just a dialogue between present and past but between the intersections of very small stories (what my great-grandmother did and what her father did, and so on) with very big stories (what the New Zealand Company did, what the British Empire did).

In her reflections on doing Aboriginal family history, Maria Nugent explains that: 'Aboriginal family history is always more than family history … it is always implicitly, sometimes explicitly, engaged with other historical narratives, both the local and national level and possibly even the global level.'[27] For an Aboriginal Australian, then, doing family history entails coming to terms with two related wrongs, 'the wrongs in the past (history-as-the-past) and the wrongs of how the past has been represented (history-as-the-past-represented).'

Perhaps all family historians – indigenous or not – confront these related wrongs as they burrow away in the past and learn how often individual stories contradict national ones. Yet the supposed smallness or narrowness of the pasts pursued by genealogists is limiting. Australian historian Graeme Davison writes that the domain of the genealogist is essentially private and it connects only tenuously with the concerns of national or international history. Doing family history, Davison argues, 'speaks not to our sense of historical significance but to our need for personal identity'.[28] Indeed, it is sometimes argued that the personal connection with the past provided by family history blinds people to the bigger picture. Many Australians and New Zealanders feel an intense attachment to relatives who fought in the First World War, and academic historians such as Joy Damousi have analysed how the 'merging of military and family history' has led to a strong investment in a nationalist, militarised past that resists necessary 'historical analysis'.[29]

Genealogists may be searching for identity, for glory or infamy, or for a place in a militarised story of the nation; they may be writing small, private, emotional and anti-analytical history. But the stories people unearth about their ancestors are powerful markers of identity in the present. As Alexis Wright suggests in her essay on family secrets, these 'little stories' resist, very powerfully, any attempt at intervention from 'big stories', such as official apologies for historical injustice, that might be imposed from outside the frame of the family. This is precisely why researchers should pay attention to them. What is a nation, really, aside from a collection of families? As Tania Evans has put it, in an article that urges academic historians to engage seriously with what genealogists are doing: 'Big pictures are constructed using lots of little people'.[30]

But the multiple Parihaka apologies – both the earlier non-negotiated ones and far more meaningful recent ones – suggest there is a disconnect between what the Crown says about the past, supposedly on behalf of the nation, and what ordinary people say about it inside their homes.

Is this disconnect merely a PR problem?

Employees of the Crown work with iwi employees (actually, more likely iwi volunteers) to research and write deeds of settlement, including negotiated historical accounts. The accounts are peer reviewed by independent eminent historians. The late Alan Ward reviewed the Taranaki deed. Often this work builds on the work already done by the Waitangi Tribunal or earlier commissions of inquiry like the Sim Commission – years and years of work, hundreds of deposits in bulging document banks, dozens of hearings and research reports, tears and drama, performances and encounters, thousands of cups of tea. The deeds are signed and published on the Office of Treaty Settlements' website, minus footnotes (fully referenced versions are available on request), and then what? Do 'people' – that is, people who are not employees of the Crown or members of mandated iwi negotiating teams, or deeply curious iwi members like myself – read them? Do schools teach them? Do textbooks refer to them? Or is the Office of Treaty Settlements' website a place to both reveal and quarantine infectious material? Would better education allow these negotiated histories on the website to start shaping the histories told and felt in homes?

DOMESTIC HISTORY VERSUS NATIONAL HISTORY

While Māori in Taranaki have repeatedly demonstrated the connections between past and present, some Pākehā resent any reminders of contact or conflict that might unsettle cherished stories of faith, heritage and pioneering decency. Several examples demonstrate this well. A few weeks before the opening of the Taranaki War exhibition in 2010, local and international Anglican dignitaries were in New Plymouth for the consecration of St Mary's Cathedral – the first new Anglican cathedral anywhere in the world in the past eighty years.[31] White settlers built the church in 1840 and Te Ātiawa leader Sir Paul Reeves, a former Archbishop of New Zealand, reminded readers that some Māori saw St Mary's, with all its attachments and flags, as a garrison church. Armaments were stored there. A parishioner took issue with Sir Paul's comments. In a letter to the editor, Connie Jones wrote:

St Mary's was never associated with Parihaka but now we have been taken over by Maori hierarchy like Tiki Raumati poking his nose in ... The 1860s wars (in which my grandfather George Henry Herbert fought as a Redcoat) has nothing to do with Parihaka. Also our new Dean, Jamie Allen, has been hoodwinked by Maori activists within Taranaki that we now have to apologise for some obscure wrongs perpetrated by the colonials.[32]

The correspondent ended her letter by saying she was 'appalled' that Tiki Raumati had been appointed Archdeacon, and that Raumati and others associated with Parihaka were 'infiltrating our beautiful new cathedral' and 'trying to rewrite our heritage'. Connie Jones was outraged, yet all she had to do was look at the walls of the church she obviously loves to find connections between the wars of the 1860s and the establishment of Parihaka Pā in 1866 as a refuge for Māori whose land had been confiscated after the wars.[33] The church is decorated with paintings of the coats of arms of various regiments that fought against Taranaki people in the wars.

The complaint about having to 'apologise for some obscure wrongs' was slotted into the letter after its author had explained her understanding of the history of the church ('built long before the 1860s Land Wars') and, by extension, of Taranaki itself. She was angry about Anglican leaders' plans to apologise, and saw this as an affront to her heritage. Māori history and Māori remembrances, she suggested, burden Pākehā.

This view is quite commonplace. In her survey of apologies in Australia, Canada, New Zealand and the United States, Melissa Nobles notes that opinion polls show 'polarization on Māori issues' – a finding that suggests 'the Waitangi Tribunal has not produced a reconciled political community'.[34] To support this contention, she cites a review of a book about the Treaty of Waitangi in which the reviewer, Philip Temple, complains that Pākehā 'are required to carry the moral burden' for historical injustice; they are 'exhausted' by this and resentful about the 'successes' of the Waitangi Tribunal process. Temple writes that 'the Treaty has come to be seen … as a one-way street, a document that enables Maori to claim and receive apologies and compensation from a largely Pakeha government without reciprocation, let alone thanks'.[35]

But Connie Jones does not appear to be carrying a moral burden about the actions of her Red Coat grandfather or about the war insignia that decorates her church. The burden, shame and exhaustion wrought by Taranaki's past is carried, overwhelmingly, by Māori, not Pākehā. Even so, in 2015 it was Pākehā residents of New Plymouth who claimed they were victims of racism because their council had voted to set up a Māori ward seat.[36]

In 2014 New Plymouth Mayor Andrew Judd, a

Pākehā, suggested iwi representatives get speaking and voting rights on New Plymouth District Council standing committees. The council voted against this, but did decide – by a small minority – to set up a Māori ward seat. Two councillors quit in protest and in 2015 a 'citizens initiated referendum' voted overwhelmingly against the proposals (23,338 residents voted; 83 per cent of them were against a Māori seat). Judd said he had been spat on in the supermarket for backing the Māori ward. His optometry business also suffered. In 2016 Judd announced he would not seek another term as mayor, and on 17 June he led a peace hīkoi from the mayor's office to Parihaka.

In interviews, Judd describes himself as a recovering racist. 'I would spend most of my life deflecting. I'd say "I'm not racist, we've got a treaty, we're paying them out, what's their problem, they don't get over it, don't improve themselves, they are all in jail, what's wrong with them, they are all savages,"' he told *One News* in May 2015. Judd may be in recovery, but the results of the citizens' referendum indicate that many others are not even aware they might have a problem.

'TE WHAKAMĀ'
The strongest evidence to refute Pākehā claims of victimhood and moral burden in Taranaki is encoded in a primary source that is now at least ninety years

old. 'Te Whakamā' (referred to in Chapter 3) was one of two historical records that Taranaki people presented to the 1926–27 government-appointed Sim Commission on confiscated lands at a sitting in Wellington. The deed of settlement between Ngāti Mutunga and the Crown explains that the waiata, 'Te Whakamā', and the ngeri (chant), 'Ko Waitara', record the experience of Ngāti Mutunga and other northern Taranaki iwi in relation to both the original confiscation legislation (the New Zealand Settlements Act 1863) and the commission's findings on the Taranaki wars, including the invasion of Parihaka.[37]

'Ko Waitara' is about the town where the Taranaki wars started in 1860 (it is also included in the Taranaki iwi deed). 'Waitara, Waitara/This was the day the land was lost/And the people were killed/What should become of us?' 'Te Whakamā' is about embarrassment and shame.

The waiata is reproduced in Māori accompanied by an English translation. As we have seen, the first few lines in English read: 'Such is the shame its conclusion will not be achieved./We the people will continue/This world inflicts a realm of pain extending far into the past/Display it all for the occasion before us.' The waiata talks specifically about the leaders at Parihaka and tells the audience that the raukura (albatross feather) worn by the performers is a sign of allegiance to the peaceful teachings of Te Whiti and Tohu. The song ends by reminding listeners of the great wrongs committed in the name of a Christian God, and that Parihaka's leaders offered an alternative: 'The clothes of the people are torn asunder, let/calm be spread through the world/As an ultimate peace upon the land/So that the actions of the prophets, Jesus and his apostles may ease off/Te Whiti and his children strove so they may/stand strong in the midst of conflict.'

Even in translation, this waiata indicates what might be wrong with an apology as a way of coming to terms with the past. Thompson argues that there are two kinds of discourses around wrongdoing or reparation. The first is legalistic and is concerned with 'rights and obligations, restoration and compensation'. The second is theological, 'concerned with apology, forgiveness, contrition, atonement and reconciliation'.[38] An apology invokes Christian ideas of good and evil, salvation and damnation, the heavenly and the earthly; yet in 'Te Whakamā', Ngāti Mutunga condemn Christianity and the things done in the name of 'Jesus and his apostles', and offer Te Whiti as an alternative to conflict. For people at Parihaka, Christianity was the source of problems.

Moving away from questions of faith, the English version of the waiata indicates that the war crimes committed by the Crown in the nineteenth century were so great that non-Māori could never make up for them. In this frame, an apology is pointless, mainly because the shame is so great it can never be 'concluded'. But the translation of the song also suggests that the confiscation of land, the imprisonment of people, the ransacking of Parihaka were intended to destroy Taranaki Māoridom. Yet even this extreme action had self-evidently failed because here, in front of the commission, were Ngāti Mutunga people singing 'E mahi tātou ake e te iwi/We the people will continue'.

However, as so often happens, quite a bit was lost in translation. I asked Pou Temara to look at the waiata. Did he think, as I did, that it is saying non-Māori will never be able to make amends for 'the things they did to the Māori people in the olden days'?

Temara started to read the Māori words. 'This song is about Māori shame and Taranaki shame at being landless,' he said. He continued to read: 'E whaiwhaia nei e te ao he ao koha rā e/kupu tautoro mua', which is translated in the deed as: 'This world inflicts a realm of pain extending far into the past.' Temara said the translation was incomplete. 'This word, whaiwhaia, is connected with mākutu.' In his opinion, the line compares confiscation with a curse, and it explains that Taranaki people 'cursed the world' because they had lost their land. But the line also expresses the feeling that 'we are cursed because we are landless'.

I was stunned. The translation, and the English-language preamble ('this song is about the embarrassment and shame "tauiwi" should have for the terrible things they did to the Māori people in the old days'), direct the reader to see a meaning in the song about ongoing Pākehā culpability. Temara's interpretation was quite different. In a typically oblique Taranaki Māori way, the waiata has a deeper, hidden meaning. By looking for these other meanings, people can turn around their understandings of past events and gain new insights into the process of reconciliation from an indigenous as well as a Crown perspective.

From the moment of invasion, Taranaki people told stories that turned events around. 'Te Piukara', the song sung by the victims of war, points out that the invading force 'lost' because the non-violence of the people at Parihaka prevented the soldiers from firing even a single shot. This work of turning events around continued in the early twentieth century as Taranaki doctor and politician Māui Pōmare (a child survivor of the raid on Parihaka) was among those who pushed for an inquiry into confiscated land. His efforts were held in such esteem that the Taranaki Maori Trust Board commissioned a carved house at Waitara (now Ōwae Marae, built on the site of Manukorihi) in his honour. The project was organised and supervised by Āpirana Ngata. Visitors to the whare whakairo walk beneath the carved figure of Māui-tikitiki-a-Taranga and beneath him is another tiki, Māui Pōmare, 'who fished out of the troublous ocean of racial conflict and misunderstanding the fish, which is the Taranaki Maori Trust Fund, the tardy requital of 1936, of the Waitara injustice of 1859'.[39] Via his friendship with Ta'isi Olaf Nelson, the businessman and Samoan independence movement leader, Pōmare planted Parihaka's ideas of non-violent resistance into the heart of the Samoan Mau movement. (Mau were described as the Te Whitis of Samoa.)[40]

At Parihaka, a tiny few kept alive the memory of waiata and poi and maintained the tradition of monthly meetings. Dick Scott's *The Parihaka Story* was self-published in 1954 with the help of some of te mōrehu at Parihaka. In the early 1970s Parihaka people asked him to update the book. *Ask That Mountain*, a revised version with a striking cover picture of Mt Taranaki by New Plymouth artist Michael Smither, was published in 1975.

By then, 'the Parihaka aunties', along with people like Ruka Broughton and Te Miringa Hōhaia, began to revive the songs and traditions of Parihaka to build up and amplify the mana. This work was part of a bigger revival and renewal, the period when, as Peter Moeahu has put it, 'the gardens of success were planted. The seeds of Kohanga Reo, Māori radio, Māori television, Māori incorporations,

Treaty settlements, improved Māori health, improved Māori education, and reduced Māori offending were sown'.[41] In Taranaki, Te Reo o Taranaki Trust was set up to restore our language within the rohe. Parihaka hosted significant large hui in the 1980s and 1990s, such as the National Work Co-op hui (1985), Te Ataarangi (1990) and Taura Whiri i te reo Māori Kura Reo (2004).

In 2000, after seven years of planning and work, Māori and Pākehā joined together to create *Parihaka: The Art of Passive Resistance*, the successful millennium exhibition at Wellington's City Gallery and accompanying award-winning book. In 2005, Te Miringa Hōhaia presided over the first peace festival held at Parihaka, an annual event that welcomed performers and guests from around the world. The festival was held annually for the next five years. In 2010 the drum that was used by the military was the drum that welcomed the Prime Minister and his entourage to a sign documents to initiate settlement talks. In 2012 Paora Joseph's documentary film *Tātarakihi – The Children of Parihaka* followed a group of Taranaki children on a hīkoi to the South Island jails where their ancestors were imprisoned. Through festivals, books, art, song and political activism and more, Taranaki people are repaying 'the bad with the good' and so lifting the burden of shame. As the final line of the Parihaka legacy statement declares:

'Ka haepapa i tōu reo, ka whakahaere tikanga koe mō te kino kia mate i te pai. Should your voice be abolished, you will use tikanga to respond to the hatred, overcoming it with kindness.'[42]

OVER TO YOU

There are multiple approaches to thinking about historical injustice and the suffering that flows from terrible events such as the confiscation of Taranaki and invasion of Parihaka. I acknowledge the importance of the work performed by the Waitangi Tribunal and the sincerity of the official apologies for te pāhua, particularly the most recent ones to Taranaki iwi (2015) and He Puanga Haeata (2017). I further acknowledge the taonga (such as tribal waiata) contained in Tribunal archives and in the deed of settlement documents published by the Office of Treaty Settlements, but this work might be considered marginal, in some ways, to the enormity of the labour within Māori families to overcome shame and sorrow.

The chair of the Parihaka Papakainga Trust, Tina Mason, and former chair Puna Wano-Bryant, have said that He Puanga Haeata has restored the mana of Parihaka and created a foundation for rebuilding relationships between the Crown and Parihaka.[43] The people who live at Parihaka now will write their own future. I am not the one to tell the story of how He Puanga Haeata was finally achieved. It is up to others to explore the significance of various statements in the 2017 Crown apology, including the emphatic acknowledgment that troops raped and molested women and girls. As Puna Wano-Bryant told RNZ, 'The women and the rape of the women, their story was silenced because of the shame that goes along with that act.'[44]

The reconciliation ceremony and accompanying Bill are further good examples of how Māori have beaten shame, victimhood and disadvantage by turning around understandings of historical events and so easing 'the realm of pain' inflicted by confiscation and marginalisation. The intimate, whānau-centred nature of this work provides a model that all New Zealanders might follow. There are encouraging signs that this is starting to happen.

In 2014, Australian actor Rebecca Gibney featured on the ancestry-based reality TV show *Who Do You Think You Are?* Researchers discovered that Gibney's ancestor James Way was a member of the Armed Constabulary force that invaded Parihaka; Gibney went to Parihaka to apologise. RNZ reported that descendants of John Hall, prime minister at the time Parihaka was invaded, and of William Rolleston, who made the declaration to invade, as well as descendants of John Bryce, the Minister of Native Affairs who led the invasion, and of members of the Armed Constabulary attended the 2017 reconciliation ceremony and expressed their remorse.[45]

The government is not the people. The Crown can keep saying sorry in Taranaki – let's hope that the inevitable apology for taking Ngā Maunga o Taranaki, Pouākai me Kaitake will be the last one – but until everyone else starts engaging with the extraordinary history-making work of Tribunal reports and settlements, then these apologies may not have the lasting impact that either iwi or the Crown would like. In 1879 Te Whiti explained to Koro Charles and the journalist Croumbie-Brown that the government ruled the people. 'We do not complain of the people, but of the Government,' Te Whiti said. 'I am quite sure that if the people had the power we would have justice done.'[46]

Will people step up now and take the time to learn, know and feel the history of the places they call home?

5. THE TRANSLATOR

Who am I to write this book? I am an expert on the archive of the world's most famous and divisive second-wave feminist. I do not live at Parihaka. I do not live in Taranaki. I don't even live in New Zealand. When I look out my window, I see a date palm and a fig tree, seven pelicans flying by. When I walk the dog, a cockie says hello from its cage. The trees in my streets have grey trunks and pale-green leaves. My mountain is a photograph on my desk. My sea is an echo in my ears when I lie in bed at night. My skin is not brown. My first and only language is English. I am not an authority on the New Zealand wars. I am not an authority on Taranaki. I am not an eminent historian. I've never worked for the Waitangi Tribunal or the Office of Treaty Settlements or the Crown Forestry Rental Trust. I've never worked for an iwi entity, pre- or post-settlement. In 2012 I did spend some months scoping out a history of Treaty settlements for the Ministry of Culture and Heritage, and for a time I was encyclopedic on that topic. I have a doctorate from an excellent Australian university and I've written many scholarly essays, but I am no longer an academic. I am not even employed if the definition of employment is performing tasks in return for money. Yet I have proceeded with this work.

I had a sob story to back up the original mandate from Te Miringa Hōhaia. I was the grieving daughter of a direct descendant of a Parihaka ploughman. The dead were in my favour.

Tare Wakarere, also known as Tare Wakawe, also known as Tare Warahi. In an appendix of the Taranaki deed of settlement, Tare Warahi (Charles Wallace) is named as one of the 182 ploughmen who were arrested between 30 June and 31 July 1879. Koro Charles, my father's great-grandfather, was my paepae, the place from which I had authority to speak. When I read the Taranaki deed in 2015, I was astonished and deeply moved to see the names of all the ploughmen and fencers. I was especially astonished to see Charles. I had not known. In April 2018 I asked iwi historian Hēmi Sundgren (now head of Te Kotahitanga o Te Atiawa Trust) how he had found the men. He told me he had worked with John Armstrong, a historian at the Office of Treaty

Settlements. Further astonishment. This was a collaborative effort?

Working together with paper archives and digitised nineteenth-century newspapers, Sundgren (Taranaki iwi) and Armstrong (Crown) arrived at a thick volume bound in peeling teal linen. The spine, which is cracked at the base, is bound in soft brown leather and the words 'Prison Register' are embossed on it in gold. You need two hands to lift this record and it's probably a good idea to brace your pelvic floor as well. A pink label inside the marbled front cover informs the reader that this volume was printed and bound in 1874 by Robert Burrett, a wholesale stationer established in 1864 on the corner of Molesworth and Willis streets, Wellington. Burrett operated 'by special Appointment to His Excellency the Governor'. On the top of one page of this large volume, Burrett printed the words 'Registered Description of Prisoners'. On the facing page the sentence was completed: 'Confined in the Gaol at New Plymouth, NZ'. Underneath this, Burrett created twenty-one headings for columns that a policeman would fill out when a prisoner arrived at the gaol. Name. Age. Size. Colour of (hair, eyes, complexion). Marks. Religion. Country where born. Education. Trade or Calling. Date of Admission. Crime. And more.

The New Plymouth Prison Register was

custom made in Wellington in 1874 and sent north. In New Plymouth, the jailer made his first entry in 1875 and the last, in a flamboyant purple pencil, in March 1885. That year was stumps for the Armed Constabulary; in 1886, the New Zealand Police was established. No need for 'armed constabulary' anymore. No need for guns now that the war of conquest was won. The register was useless. It represented the old power. It had the wrong headings at the top of each page. Most of the pages were never even filled in. Even so, no one threw the register out. It sat on a shelf in the New Plymouth prison, waiting. Then the century ticked over. It sat for many more decades then, at some stage, perhaps around the time the New Zealand Police was getting ready to celebrate its centenary, or perhaps a little earlier, the register – nicely aged and historic now – was transferred from New Plymouth to the Prison Staff College, a national training centre for prison officers set up in Upper Hutt in 1972.

My time with the Greer Archive taught me how to read a record, how to consider the people who made it and then the people who cared for it and described it, and how to analyse this information as an important part of the record's provenance and meaning. As Archives New Zealand notes: 'The College has collected a variety of material from prisons all around the country for use as staff training aids. Hence the records they have transferred to National Archives often consist of early prison records, rather than records from the College itself."[1]

In 1995 the new Department of Corrections took over the administration of the Prison College, and the register was subsequently transferred to the custodianship of the National Archives at Pipitea. Almost two more decades passed. If you order the record, as I did, you will see the agency code is ABGU – which stands for Department of Corrections, Prison Staff College – and an accession number, W3777, which tells you these are prison records. And when you open this prison record, item ID R18388482, you will see exactly how New Zealand, the Governor, the Crown – via its agent, perhaps not even a constable, maybe a mere clerk, a functionary working at a jail in New Plymouth – imposed itself on Taranaki. This enormous power, this crushing power, this power that was hidden inside some headings printed at the top of the columns and hidden inside the shapes made on the page by some constable with his fountain pen (or hidden in the blanks where he could not even be bothered to make a mark), is shameful. Let the power register. Hang your head.

Take a guess what the constable wrote underneath the heading 'Trade or Calling' for the first Parihaka ploughmen who were arrested and registered as prisoners of New Plymouth jail in

June 1879? He wrote: Labourer. And underneath the heading Education: Cannot. And when armed constables started arresting twenty or thirty men a day, he wrote the man's name, his age, the date. Nothing more. Country where born: blank. Education: blank. Trade or Calling: blank. Crime for which committed: blank. Sentence: blank. Articles received from Prisoner, and Signature of Prisoner on Admission: blank.

Cannot read? Cannot write? Will not? Or is the word 'cannot' referring to the constable and the colonial power he represents, the power that cannot – will not – understand the first thing about the higher education that the man standing before him has received in another world. Wānanga. Cannot. Whaikōrero. Cannot. Whakapapa. Cannot. Waiata. Cannot. Ruruku. Cannot. Karakia. Cannot.

Or are some of the blank spaces a case of another 'will not'? On 9 July 1879, in a story headlined 'The Ploughing Mania', the *Patea Mail* reported that Whakawiria, one of the men arrested for ploughing, was asked to sign his name but refused. 'Whakawiria said – I will not obey – I feel angry. Write it yourself. (This was to show contempt for the Court and Government).' This phrase, an explanatory observation from the reporter, or translator (Koro Charles), is used twice in the article. 'Whakawiria here showed his contempt for the Court and our power.'

'You speak to me, the lord of the land. I am your lord. Listen to your lord,' Whakawiria said. 'I am not going to talk of the things of heaven, but of Tohu – the lord of the ploughing, of Parihaka, and Tohu is lord of all. We are ploughing the belly of the Government. I have only the one word to turn you off my blanket.'

Keep turning the pages of the register. There are very many names. Mass civil disobedience – an administrative nightmare! Not to mention a space issue. Where did they put all these men? What did they feed them?

Before the Parihaka arrests, most of the prisoners registered at the New Plymouth gaol were men and women who were born overseas – Scotland, Ireland, England and Italy – and every column next to their names is filled in. The charges are comprehensive. Vagrancy, manslaughter, deserting family, larceny, deserting child, drunkenness, insanity, assault, burglary, arson, lunacy and rape (one charge only, registered in 1884). The names of the people born overseas are allowed to stand on their own, but the names of men from Parihaka all have a qualifier (a Native). As in: Te Whiti (a Native), 53, 5 foot 10, Black, Black, Dark, 2 fingers off right hand. Religion: Pro (for Protestant). Birth place: N.Z. Education: blank. Trade or calling: Chief or Labourer. Date of admission to gaol: 12 November 1881. Crime for which Committed: blank.

Or: Tohu (a Native), 51, 5 foot 11, Black, Black, Dark, 2 fingers off left hand. Religion: Pro. Birth place: N.Z. Education: blank. Trade or calling: Chief or Labourer. Date of admission: 12 November 1881. Crime for which committed: blank.

Also: Titokowaru (a Native). Date of admission: 23 November 1881. Blind in right eye. Trade or calling: Chief or Labourer.

I photographed the pages of the register as I went and scribbled impressions in my notebook. *It's just a total feeling of overwhelm,* I've written in pencil above the names of the three rangatira. Stopped work and said prayer.

The extent of the arrests is horrific, I wrote.

The worst thing about these later arrests (1880) is that these men are in their 40s, 50s and 60s. (Though I also took photos of the names of arrested boys who were 16 and 17.) *No note what happened to these men arrested in 1879, where they were sent, for how long, but by July 1880 that has changed. Longer note says sent to Lyttelton gaol.*

In the column marked 'Sentence' the clerk has just written a number, counting up how many arrested this day.

The column labelled 'Articles received from prisoner' is filled in for non-Māori people (long coat, pipe and tobacco, hat and boots, stockings, petticoats) but is blank for ploughmen and fencers. *Nothing taken from Parihaka men. Was this because there was nothing left to take? Or were items taken and not recorded?*

I also noted down the details for Tare Wakarere, aka Tare Wakawe, aka Tare Warahi, and photographed from several angles the page where his name was written. *Is this Charles??*

I mentioned to my family that I had seen the register with all the prisoners' names, including Charles's, but when I got back to Melbourne and consulted Aunty Raumahora's whakapapa book, I was unsure. Aunty wrote: 'Charles Taare took no part in the wars mainly because of his youth but principally because his kinsfolk on his mother's side were fighting against the Pakeha.' When the first war started in Taranaki in 1860, Charles was only twelve; by the 1870s he was a man, old enough to decide for himself. His first child, William Ellerslie Wallace II, was born in 1879, the year men were arrested for ploughing. Aunty wrote that after 'hostilities ceased' Charles joined the Armed Constabulary and 'served for some years up and down the Taranaki coast maintaining peace and order in a still turbulent district'. Yes, I did consider leaving this piece of information out.

When I began to compose my mihi at the start of Chapter 2, I typed: *Hannah's father, Taare Warahi (Charles Wallace), was born at Te Aro Pa in 1848. In 1879 Koro Charles was arrested for ploughing land occupied by settlers near Parihaka.* I wanted the sentence to be true, the deed appeared to say it was true, but I felt that it was not. I spent the rest of the morning searching through Papers Past, the collection of digitised newspapers at the National Library of New Zealand, and that is where I found what Koro Charles was really up to then. Koro was the court-appointed translator for at least one hearing for Parihaka ploughmen (he translated the words of Whakawiria I quoted above), and in late August 1879 he was allowed to bring *Lyttelton Times* journalist Samuel Croumbie-Brown on to Parihaka.

After the ploughing arrests, journalists rushed to Taranaki to cover the big story. Croumbie-Brown was in Hāwera, trying to find a way to get to Parihaka and score an interview with Te Whiti. 'I determined that if the Government would not march on Parihaka, I would,' he wrote in 'Among the Maoris in the North Island', an article filed in Wellington on 1 September and published several days later in *The Star*, a sister paper to the *Lyttelton Times*. But Te Whiti had refused to speak to other men of 'high rank'. Croumbie-Brown was also worried about the 'sullen and dangerous' character of some Parihaka residents, namely Hīroki, the man accused of murdering a surveyor. 'But these difficulties were as nothing compared to that of obtaining the right sort of interpreter,' he wrote.

There were men who *volunteered* to go *con amore* (suspicious – very!); there were men who demanded exorbitant pay; there were men qualified but who 'funked on it'... it was only through the kind offices of friends who took a deep interest in the matter that I at last procured the services of Charles Wallace, a half-caste, who not only has the reputation of being an excellent interpreter, but bears a character above suspicion as far as double dealing between the races. I will only say of him here that he served me diligently and faithfully and at critical points of my arguments with Te Whiti displayed rare tact and quickness of judgment.

Is it a good or a bad sign that the journalist trusted Charles? Was Charles the 'right sort of interpreter' only in the eyes of white settlers? Was he two-faced or was he fair to both races? Was Croumbie-Brown someone who could be trusted to make that assessment? What did Koro Charles's relatives at Parihaka think? What did his wife Margaret think at home in Pātea? She was only seventeen, either heavily pregnant or already nursing a new baby.

The journalist and the interpreter rode together for two days across the Waimate Plains. The journalist carried a revolver but he left it behind at Ōpunake because 'the nearer we approached Parihaka, the more cordial the demeanor of the people'. There were two hundred whare at Parihaka, twelve hundred people 'at the lowest computation', and enough food, water and fuel to last a very long siege. The journalist had been a war correspondent in the American Civil War and had covered the raids by the Fenian Brotherhood (an Irish republican organisation) on British forts in Canada. He had an eye for detail that was relevant to the military, not to mention a keen understanding of the business of freelancing. War stories would sell, and several years later Croumbie-Brown defied the press ban to sneak into Parihaka and provide an eyewitness account of the invasion.

After a pōwhiri, Te Whiti, his wife, Tohu and 'the principal people to the number of about 50' assembled in 'Te Whiti's whare'. Perhaps they met in Miti Mai Te Arero, the first European-style building at Parihaka, built about then under the supervision of Te Whetu Moeahu? Sketches made by Private James Ledger, a member of the invading force in 1881, describe 'a European house erected to receive the Governor had he wished to visit Te Whiti'. Its name means 'to defiantly protrude one's tongue'. It would be a fitting place for the encounter.

Speaking through Koro Charles, the journalist says: 'I have come from Christchurch, the large city of the island of green stone. I am a man of a newspaper – a newspaper that all men know. We who reside in the other island search for the reasons of the troubles that exist between the European tribe and the Maori tribe. We want to find out if the wrong is with the Government, or with the ordinary European, or with the newspapers of the North Island.'

Te Whiti doubts the journalist. He tells Koro Charles to tell Croumbie-Brown that he suspects he is a government official, not a newspaper man. Te Whiti tells Koro Charles to advise Croumbie-Brown to study, to wait a little while. The journalist tells Koro Charles to tell Te Whiti that he has studied the situation from every point of view, except Parihaka's. He has come to Parihaka so he can stand and look at it, as Koro Charles puts it so well. But Te Whiti is getting restless.

Te Whiti says: But my talking to you will be like talking over a mountain, because you will not hear it (meaning that I would hear his voice, but would not understand the figurative speech of the Maori).

Croumbie-Brown says: Not so, Te Whiti, because there is between us a man (the interpreter) through whom your voice to me and my voice to you go, and everything is made clear to us.

Te Whiti says: Yes, that is very true.

Koro Charles says all of those things and more. What I wish my children and nieces and nephews to know, and what I so wish my father had known, is that their Koro was permitted to stand in front of one of New Zealand's greatest political and spiritual leaders and listen. I wish them to know that their

Koro was a special sort of listener. Because of who he was, because of how he was raised, because of where he was born, because of who his parents and grandparents and great-grandparents were, he was able to turn one set of sounds into another, and so he could make words pass through a mountain.

Creator, keeper, translator, interpreter, intermediary: I recognise Charles (and the reporter whose words he echoed) because I recognise myself. Shared DNA. This is what he did. That is what they did. This is what I am now doing, listening and thinking, translating and interpreting, witnessing, taking notes, creating this new record that you are now holding in your hands. Not a straight line, a koru.

RECORD-KEEPERS

I searched the Puke Ariki catalogue for Parihaka, and dozens of digitised colour photographs popped up. I hadn't seen them before: 1962, a row of kuia outside a rotting house, singing, serious, then giggling, hamming it up for the camera; undated 35mm slide, men and women gutting a pig, laughing; 1963, a little girl in red rompers and a red and white top dances in front of a line of people carrying plates of food for a tangi; undated, hui, Humbers, Ford Escorts, Austin A40s, a VW are parked on the grass, and in the foreground are two blokes in shorts, knee-high white socks and fawn jerseys; 1969, children playing in a sandbox at Tohu's marae; undated, people sitting in the sun on the porch and lawn at Pae Pae, Tito's family home; 1960s, builders work at reconditioning Te Niho o Te Ātiawa house; 1972, guys lean on shovels next to a hāngī pit; 1970s, four kids playing in a swimming hole. Dozens of photographs of buildings too, many of them in ruins. Ditto for photos of old drays and ploughs. Not so joyful, those ones.

Rigby Allan took the pictures. He was director of the Taranaki Museum from 1961 until his retirement in 1974, and between 1954 and 1977 visited Parihaka dozens of times. A black and white photograph from October 1974 is evidence that Allan was welcomed at Parihaka and the community valued his efforts to learn about the place and to document the ongoing family and community life there. Sally Karena, Rigby Allan, Netta Wharehoka, Iwimarie Maruwhenua, Ngahina Okeroa, Richard Wharehoka, Miriama Wharehoka and Matarena Marjorie Rau-Kupa are gathered around a package. 'The photo was taken during the presentation of the travelling rug to Rigby Allan by the Parihaka pā committee,' the caption says.

In April 2018 I went to Taranaki to spend some time with the mountain and visit relatives. I asked Puke Ariki about Rigby's photographs. Did he make notes as well? Archivist Lucy Macfarlane presented me with three boxes of unlisted material

(Rigby Allan Notes, ARC2007-233/1 Allan, Rigby M9/2/1). Two contained folders; the other box held about seventeen reporter's notebooks and an old audiotape. Most of the notebooks documented Allan's regular trips to Parihaka, often on 7 November, the day Parihaka commemorates te pāhuatanga. He was there in 1973 and his notes reveal a community buzzing with creative energy. Artists were almost tripping over each other. 'Michael King with his TV vans and crew also there,' Allan wrote of 7 November 1973.

They had permission to film any time but the sacred day. Michael Smither arrived as I was leaving. Bell Block school in residence for 2 nights and 3 days. Bruce Hammond going out daily. John Ford went with me and took plans for decorations he hopes to have approval to apply. Poppy Bailey from Waitara also there with a group of children at Pae Pae. At Te Niho same day Netta Wharehoka, Sally Karena, Marg [Matarena] Rau, Ina [Ngahina] Okeroa all in kitchen … before meal Te Niho people went down to Kapui marae while Tonganui, Moses Wharepouri and Ken Ranhi spoke to crowd … some criticism of Pakeha people generally. When meal announced Maoris were told to go in first then Pakehas. James Mack of Waikato Museum presented a large Parihaka photo on marae at Kapui they left it on the ground. Marg [Matarena] took it to Te Niho. Tuhoe folk stayed the night on Te Niho.

To translate some of this: The four women in the kitchen at Te Niho are 'the Parihaka aunties', whose skill as teachers of poi and waiata helped spark the renewal of Parihaka. Whero o Te Rangi ('Poppy') Bailey, who was also revered for her knowledge of poi, weaving, waiata and te reo, grew up at Parihaka. Michael King was the writer and interviewer for a six-part television documentary *Tangata Whenua* (1974) directed by Barry Barclay (Ngāti Apa). Painter Michael Smither was designing the cover for Dick Scott's *Ask That Mountain: The Story of Parihaka* (1975). John Ford (Ngāti Raukawa ki Kapiti) was an eminent carver and painter who went on to be exhibited at the Metropolitan Museum of Art New York and the British Museum. James Mack was curator of *Taranaki Saw It All* (1973) at the Waikato Museum and Art Gallery. 'Kapui' is the house Rangi Kapuia opened in 1927. I don't know about the other people or the kaupapa of the Tūhoe delegation. Perhaps Bruce Hammond was the painter Bill Hammond?

Parihaka's buildings were rotting and its amenities were dilapidated. Rates notices came but the services did not follow. Parihaka serviced itself. Even so, the settlement was a creative generator, an epicentre of artistic energy, a place with massive centripetal and centrifugal force.[2]

A couple of years earlier, on 28 May 1971, Allan went to a meeting about the future of Parihaka at the home of 'Mr and Mrs Sharlands' in Westown, New Plymouth. 'The meeting was chaired by Dr Tony

Ruakere of New Plymouth Hospital. Also present were Marg [Matarena] Rau, Richard Wharehoka of Pungarehu and his aunt Mrs Whatarau, Netta Wharehoka secretary of the Parihaka marae committee,' Allan wrote. After this meeting, Dad's friend Tony started to hunt for Dick Scott to ask him to update *The Parihaka Story*. By 30 October 1971, Allan notes: 'Dick Scott … at Parihaka. Scott about to rewrite his book so gaining more information. He has been to England and located in British Museum a full face sketch of Te Whiti …'

Wind back a little further to Allan's first folder of notes on Parihaka. It is 7 November 1956, two years after *The Parihaka Story* has come out, three years after Scott, a young communist, went to Parihaka. Scott had heard about the community when he read *Bryce v Rusden*, a notorious nineteenth-century libel case that the former Native Minister and leader of the invasion of Parihaka took against George Rusden, a historian. In his evocative introduction to *The Parihaka Story*, Scott describes a ghost town:

I arrived at the pa at dusk, unknown and unannounced. I had walked the grass streets past empty doorways and blank windows, past sagging verandahs and a fallen roof, until I reached a house that was inhabited. The big woman who came to the door was ready for help for the traveller.

Allan notes that he went to Parihaka with Mrs Raumati and Mrs Bailey. The small crowd at the feast included George Pokai, a relative of Tītokowaru whose father had been imprisoned twice, once at Port Cooper and once at Otago, for erecting fences as soldiers approached Parihaka. Pokai's uncle had also been imprisoned. Three of his sons had fought in the Second World War and one of them had been killed. Allan notes that Pokai was the only speaker after tea that day. Pokai (George Te Kahui Pokai Aitua) died in 1960 in the fire that burnt down Te Raukura, Te Whiti's house.

In 1961 Allan made at least three trips to Parihaka. On 18 June he got talking with Jim Tonganui 'who told me his mother was born the morning of Bryce's raid'.

On 7 November 1961, the eightieth anniversary of the invasion, he was back there again. Allan listened to five women from Hāwera and Ōpunake singing sacred poi songs that 'related to the suffering of the Maori people following the raid'. He mentioned that there was only one person at the commemoration that day who had witnessed the raid. He calls her 'old Mrs Okeroa'. After poi had been performed, the men were 'overcome' and wept. Moses Wharepouri and Tim Tonganui both spoke and 'thanked the women and mentioned that the remembering of the sacred poi words in itself was a feat of merit and stating that had men been entrusted with the task, they would have been forgotten long ago'.

'Old Mrs Okeroa – in another world since the house Raukura was burnt down – was the recorder (although she could neither read nor write) of all the hakas and poi for Te Whiti,' Allan writes.

And so one record-keeper reveals the work of another. The post-1970 rejuvenation of Parihaka hinged on the revival of poi and haka. These works of art are primary sources for what happened in the nineteenth century and the way Taranaki Māori interpreted these happenings. They are central to the Treaty claims and settlements processes. They have been performed at signings, quoted in oratory, and published, in both languages, in deeds. Six waiata composed around this time are published in the Taranaki deed. After the invasion, the women of Parihaka wrote and performed a poi that begins 'Muri ahiahi, As evening falls …' The Taranaki deed of settlement says the waiata 'described their experiences being raped or otherwise molested by Crown troops'. This poi was a closed record (that is, it had not been performed for decades) but Taranaki iwi decided to perform it again at the initialling of our deed at Puke Te Whiti (Pukeiti) in 2015, and the poi was also performed at Parihaka for He Puanga Haeata. Women did not report the rapes and assaults to the Armed Constabulary, but they didn't sweep the attacks under the carpet either. They created this other, more enduring record of events, and 'old Mrs Okeroa' kept the record and many others safe inside herself. While the work of Parihaka scribe Te Kāhui Kararehe has been widely acknowledged, it is time to also acknowledge the feat of merit of women like this kuia who recorded Parihaka's history by remembering its waiata, haka and poi, and the feat of merit of other kuia in Taranaki who have remembered equally powerful waiata, such as Ngāti Mutunga's 'Te Whakamā'.[3]

I talked with Mahara Okeroa about the note-books that Rigby Allan had kept. I thought they were important records but they also made me sad. There were so few people left at Parihaka when Allan started to visit, just a few survivors holding fast to the old ways. The phrases I had read came to mind.

Burnt house. One of few people left. Hand adzed totara boards rotting away. Small crowd. Only three old ladies in attendance (all living at Pah) traditional welcomes still given to visiting parties. Boarded over. Before the poi performance on marae a long skipping rope was produced and turned. A number of the old women stepped out and lasted a few skips …[4]

It was when I told Mahara about 'old Mrs Okeroa', the woman who had remembered all the Parihaka songs for Te Whiti, that he drew the koru and the straight line on the tabletop. He said those kuia had enormous will and resilience. 'The distance between me and them is this small,' he said and put his thumb and forefinger together. 'It's nothing.'

I sent him the notes I made about the Rigby

Allan papers. A few days later I got an email: 'The old Kuia Mrs Okeroa who was referred to as the only survivor of the pāhuatanga of Parihaka is my Grandmother. Her name was Te Ngoungou. Many thanks Mahara.'

He told me once that he had another name and Mahara was a substitute for this. But maybe the substitute is something more, an echo of an earlier request. Mahara! Remember. Know.

6. KO TARANAKI
TE MAUNGA

Ko Taranaki te Maunga
Ko Taranaki te iwi
Ko Taranaki te tangata
Ko te puna i heke mai ai te tangata
E kore e pau te ika unahi nui

Taranaki is the mountain
Taranaki is the tribe
Taranaki is the eponymous ancestor
The spring from which we all flow
We will never be overcome, we are like the scales of a great fish

What are Treaty settlements for? What have settlements achieved? I asked one of my senior relatives for his views and he said, 'Treaty settlements are fake news.' I nearly choked on my Pepsi Max (this kaumātua's favourite drink). He makes me laugh so much, but in this instance I don't agree.

Good news, bad news, fake news, no news, I appreciate there are many answers to the question about settlements – and the settlements outside settlements, such as He Puanga Haeata – but I can answer only for myself. Treaty settlements are not about the apologies, or the small amount of money paid out (relative to what was lost or taken), or the fiddling about with name changes and titles, or the sometimes bizarre pieces of unwanted surplus Crown land that are handed back (for Taranaki Whānui ki te Upoko o Te Ika this included an abandoned school, a hazardous nature reserve, half a car park and a nudist beach). For me, the most important and enduring thing about Waitangi Tribunal claims and settlements are the relationships they have created or exposed, and the oral, written and visual records that have been generated, unearthed, debated and shared in the process. In other words, settlements are about knowledge and they are about custodianship of this knowledge. Alongside the contemporary records generated by the Māori Land Court and its historic block order files, this knowledge is now an immense and priceless data set for us, the descendants of the old people whose homes and cultures were pulled from under their feet in the nineteenth and twentieth centuries.

This knowledge is not everything, of course, but if you come from a family like mine – one in which the only taonga left by the mid twentieth century were the pieces of paper from the Public Trustee telling you your shares in Māori land are worthless or near worthless – then it is pretty special. I feel a deep gratitude towards all the Māori and Pākehā people who worked on the Waitangi Tribunal's Taranaki Report and created the amazing 'document bank' that I can make withdrawals from whenever I like.

Knowledge beats shame. When Dad was a boy, he knew he had 'Māori blood' but not much more. He had to struggle to find out who he was and where he came from, and so did many other descendants of Koro Charles Wallace. This book, and *The Parihaka Album* before it, is possible only because of their work, along with the Māori-led land rights and language revival movements and the Treaty claims processes that both prompted and supported whānau efforts. Dad strained to learn Māori and he did learn enough to uphold tikanga in many different situations. My heart broke when I found all the bits of paper he had filed in his 'Te Reo' folder at Village at the Park; he had even kept the notes from the Kuratini course in 1986. He was so dogged. He ploughed through, undeterred by his undoubtedly idiosyncratic pronunciation. One aspect of whaikōrero he did master was the strategic cough, and he milked it.

Dad would give a blessing at the start of staff meetings at Hutt Valley Hospital, where he was a paediatrician. He set up the Māori sub-committee at the Royal Australasian College of Physicians and would do the honours there as well. When St Mary of the Angels on Boulcott Street, Wellington, re-opened after earthquake strengthening, Dad was the kaumātua who blessed the church. Dad even spoke at Waitangi once, when he accepted the John Sands medal for services to paediatrics. Afterwards, one of the locals came up to him and said of the Māori part of his oratory: 'We couldn't believe it. You just kept going!'

I have already referred to Dad's childhood, when his grandmother Hannah, Koro Charles's daughter, would take him to a coffee shop on Manners Mall and she would tell him, 'We used to be here – this is our place.' Did they know the name of the place? Te Aro, to turn towards (the mountain, Taranaki). In any case, Dad had just two scraps of knowledge – his grandmother's words, and later the mnemonic of the pā's name – but he lived long enough to see Te Aro Pā reveal itself again in 2005 when remains of whare ponga were unearthed during the construction of Bellagio/Ataahui Apartments on Taranaki Street. As my sister Hannah wrote: 'Leo – alongside other whanaunga – spent many years seeking justice for Te Aro whenua and uri of the pa. And in his final decade, one of his greatest rewards was seeing the Te Aro Pā Papakāinga on Evans Bay Parade rise up again.'

Dad and I spent a lot of time trying to find out where Koro Charles's grandfather Hēmi Parai was buried. We never found out; he was probably put to rest in the part of the Bolton Street cemetery that was dug up for the motorway. We did not discuss where Charles's mother, Arapera, might be buried, and I don't know.

It is amazing to me that my father is buried in an urupā, not a cemetery. He is wearing a tie, but Pekiara Rei also pinned a raukura on his coat. He had a bilingual Requiem Mass at St Mary's and Father Barry gave us permission to sleep next to Dad in the church the night before. Dad had set money aside to pay for James Young, the organist, and the choir, and as we carried Dad out the organ was thumping out 'Whakaaria Mai'. At the doors of the church, the singing and the organ paused and all I could hear was Jamie Tuuta chanting ancient Taranaki incantations and prayers. I offer my sincerest thanks to our relatives for the respects they paid Dad, his ancestors and his descendants at that time, and the support they offered us.

By fluke or serendipity or some other force, Dad is the first one at Opau, the new urupā at Makara that was part of the 2009 Treaty settlement between Taranaki-Te Ātiawa whānui in Wellington and the

Crown. The urupā is one thing I can wholeheartedly celebrate about the settlement.

Six months after Dad's death I returned to New Zealand. I went to see him at Opau. I told him about this book and I mentioned I was going up to Taranaki the next day. I had a schedule in mind; I hoped to sit in on a hui about the mountains – Taranaki, Pouākai and Kaitake. The record of understanding signed in December 2017 says representatives of the post-settlement entities of the eight Taranaki iwi are in negotiations to 'develop an apology and cultural redress in relation to ngā maunga' and that 'the apology and cultural redress … will not include any financial or commercial redress'.

The day after I arrived in Taranaki I borrowed my foster-sister's jeep and drove up to the car park at 'North Egmont'. I choose the loop track and started to climb, powering past the other walkers with an ease I did not know I possessed. But then I was alone and climbing down the mountain, and I ran out of breath. I was coughing and wheezing. Help me, I said to the air. I touched the trunk of a big old tree. Help me. After Dad's death, I had put certain painful things into the deep-freeze compartment of my brain, but now I was back in New Zealand they had started to thaw. I had no idea what to do.

I stared down at my feet. I was on the mountain. He has his own weather, his own time, indifferent. What am I going to do? I asked. Silence. I was alone, trudging through the mud. Wood pigeon, kererū – I heard the familiar low whooshing sound of its wings. I used to love seeing the wood pigeons in our garden at Rogan Street when I was a kid. They feasted on the strawberry tree. Now this bird was with me here. It landed on a tree up just ahead, a beauty, with luxuriant glossy green feathers and a white breast and legs, the pinhead sitting serene above the juicy body. The bird took off as I got nearer and swooped among the trees, landing again further on from me. This time, the bird let me get very close. I unzipped my backpack and took out the camera. The bird didn't move, not even when the shutter clicked. I took a couple of selfies back at the car park, and under the sweat there is pleasure and some peace.

Tracker Tilmouth talked about the enjoyment of land rights. Alexis Wright uses the phrase many times in her biography. Joy, delight and happiness are rarely part of stories around land rights. It's mostly the other stuff: alienation, loss, exclusion, degradation, frustration and poverty. Achieving the enjoyment of land rights was part of what Tracker called his vision splendid. He talked about how Aboriginal people had responded, or not, to the different policies of the successive governments they have had to deal with. It all came back to the question of 'who we are as a sovereign people – and if we are a sovereign people, please act like a sovereign people'. In other words, don't wait for someone to give you permission, to deem you worthy enough, or black enough, or traditional enough, or authentic enough, or victim enough or whatever. Act like a sovereign person now!

Tracker said: 'So you go through this process, and when you look at what has been delivered in land rights, the big question that still lies unanswered is not the acquisition of land rights, but the enjoyment of land rights. How do you enjoy being where you are?'[1]

I read *Tracker* just before my trip back to New Zealand. *Dad, enjoyment of land rights*, I've written on one page. I've written the same thing on a Post-it stuck in another page. Knowingly or unknowingly, Dad exercised a full enjoyment of land rights in Wellington and Taranaki. One of the main ways he did this was by walking. His enjoyment of Taranaki was extreme. We lived in New Plymouth in the 1970s and early 1980s, and Dad took us up the mountain many times. We climbed the tracks, crashed through the bush to catch a baby goat that we wanted to keep as a pet (Mum said no), screamed our heads off at lookouts, and followed Dad across icy slopes, decked out in top-of-the-range mountaineering gear (Charlie Brown school shoes, homemade skirts and jerseys). Dad wore knee-high socks, brown slip-on shoes, walk shorts and a jersey of flecked brown and burgundy wool.

I recall all the little details because my sister had a friend with her that day, and this girl, reasonably enough, had a panic attack as we started to skid about on the snow-encrusted slope. The walk took ages as a result. We visited Pukeiti and Dawson Falls.

Two nights before Dad died, I dreamed we were on the mountain again. I was a child, and I was wearing a woollen skirt with flowers and butterflies on it. Dad was in his thirties, still young, and he was wearing those walk shorts and long socks, his slip-on leather shoes and his flecked jumper, and we were laughing so hard. Dad was panting and gasping with laughter. 'Come on, Dad,' I shouted out to him. 'Hurry up, Dad. Follow me.' I ran ahead of him, skipping over the rocks and vines. I was as light as air and it was easy for me to breathe; the air was golden and it flowed in and out of me smoothly. In this beautiful dream, my childhood asthma was gone. I was free. I was leading Dad up the mountain, teasing him, but urging him on as well. 'Dad! Come on, silly sausage. Hurry up!' It was not so easy for Dad, he was struggling a bit, but he kept trying to catch me.

When I woke up, I felt peaceful for the first time in months. I told Mike about the dream and said I thought Dad would die soon. Much later I learned that two nights before he died, Dad had had a massive stroke. He could not see anymore, or speak. He felt no pain but his heart was still beating.

NOTES

Chapter 1

1   Rachel Buchanan, 'Beating Shame: Parihaka and the Very Long Sorry', *Te Pouhere Kōrero 6, Māori History, Māori People* (2012), pp.55–82. With thanks to editors Aroha Harris and Alice Te Punga Somerville, the two anonymous peer reviewers and the many others who helped me with this sorry mahi between 2009 and 2018.

Chapter 2

1   Raumaahora Rama-Anne Broughton, Charles Taare Warahi Wallace 1848–1932, whakapapa book, 2010, pp.13–14; S. Croumbie-Brown, 'Among the Maoris in the North Island' (from the Special Travelling Reporter of the *Lyttelton Times*), interview with Te Whiti, *The Star*, 3 September 1879.

2   Croumbie-Brown, 'Among the Maoris in the North Island'.

3   See Taranaki iwi and Te Kāhui o Taranaki Trust and The Crown, *Deed of Settlement of Historical Claims*, 5 September 2015, p.59.

4   See Rachel Buchanan, 'Orimupiko 22 and the Haze of History', *Journal of New Zealand Studies*, 16 (2013), pp. 66–78, and Rachel Buchanan, 'There's a Buried Forest on My Land', *Tell You What*, Auckland University Press, Auckland, 2015, pp.124–31.

5   Hazel Riseborough, 'A New Kind of Resistance: Parihaka and the Struggle for Peace', in Kelvin Day (ed.), *Contested Ground Te Whenua I Tohea: The Taranaki Wars 1860–1881*, Huia, Wellington, 2010, pp.231–32. See also Danny Keenan, *Te Whiti o Rongomai and the Resistance of Parihaka*, Huia, Wellington, 2015, p.19.

6   'Te Pire Haeata ki Parihaka/ Parihaka Reconciliation Bill, Te Tikanga Tuku Iho Schedule 2 Legacy Statement' written by Ruakere Hond and Hēmi Sundgren.

7   Nigel Prickett, 'Pākehā and Māori Fortifications in Taranaki, 1860–1881', in Day (ed.), *Contested Ground*, p.86.

8   Tim Ryan, 'The Māori Warrior and the British Soldier', in Day (ed.), *Contested Ground*, p.109.

9   The Strutt painting, which was on display at Te Papa in May 2018 in a very small exhibition commemorating the land wars, came to prominence

because the Govett-Brewster Gallery, New Plymouth, wants to display it in 2019. Peter Moeahu was among the senior Taranaki leaders to speak out against 'the lie' of the painting. 'Generations of New Zealanders grew up thinking the Strutt painting was a true reflection of history and that Māori were thieves and robbers,' Moeahu wrote in a letter to the editor, *Taranaki Daily News*, 30 April 2018. See also 'Jamie Tuuta and the Strutt Painting', RNZ, 1 May 2018, www.radionz.co.nz/programmes/ours/story/2018641597/jamie-tuuta-and-the-strutt-painting (accessed 7 June 2018).

10 Taranaki iwi, *Deed of Settlement*, p.20.

11 With thanks to manager Kelvin Day, Poutiaki Taonga Kararaina Te Ira and their colleagues for their assistance.

12 J.C. Sturm, 'A Tricky Business', in Te Miringa Hōhaia, Gregory O'Brien and Lara Strongman (eds), *Parihaka: The Art of Passive Resistance*, Victoria University Press, Wellington, 2001, p.205. Quoted with the permission of the Literary Estate of J.C. Sturm.

13 Taranaki iwi, *Deed of Settlement*, p.20.

14 The New Zealand Settlements Act 1863, Appendix II Confiscation Legislation, *The Taranaki Report: Kaupapa Tuatahi*, Waitangi Tribunal, Wellington, 1996, fragment from p.351.

15 The New Zealand Settlements Act 1863, *The Taranaki Report*, p.351.

16 Taranaki iwi, *Deed of Settlement*, p.22.

17 Ibid., p.26.

18 Milton Hōhaia, 'He Rerenga Kōrero': The Rape of Parihaka and Its Healing*, The New Zealand Archive of Film, Television and Sound, 29 June 1994, reference 42648, available online at ngataonga.org.nz

19 James Belich, 'Titokowaru, Riwha', *Dictionary of New Zealand Biography*, Te Ara – the Encyclopedia of New Zealand, https://teara.govt.nz/en/biographies/1t101/titokowaru-riwha (accessed 17 July 2018).

20 Titokowaru, 10 November 1881, ADUW 17906 P-NP4/1 Charge Book – January 1878–October 1884, Police Station, New Plymouth, Te Rua Mahara o te Kāwanatanga, Archives New Zealand (hereafter ANZ), Item ID: R13032434. The New

Plymouth Armed Police Force was set up in 1851 and this record is a remnant of the force's administrative infrastructure (ADUW is the agency abbreviation at ANZ).

21   Ruakere Hond, 'The Concept of Wananga at Parihaka', in Hōhaia, O'Brien and Strongman (eds), *Parihaka: The Art of Passive Resistance*, p.86.

22   Hazel Riseborough, 'Te Pāhuatanga o Parihaka', in Hōhaia, O'Brien and Strongman (eds), *The Art of Passive Resistance*, p.19.

23   Major collaborative research between Hēmi Sundgren and John Armstrong resulted in the unearthing of the names of the ploughmen and fencers arrested in the two early stages of Parihaka passive resistance protests in 1879 and 1880, and in subsequent protests, post invasion, in 1886 and 1897–98. With thanks to Hēmi and John for their assistance, including providing references to the Prison Register and Charge Book. See Taranaki iwi, Deed of Settlement, Annex 1 and 2, pp.54–59.

24   *Patea Mail*, 9 July 1879.

25   Exchange between Tuki Tuki, Parihaka, ploughman, and Farquar Finlayson, a farmer, as interpreted by Charles Wallace, *Patea Mail*, 9 July 1879.

26   S. Croumbie-Brown and Charles Wallace, 'By our special correspondent, Opunake, Te Whiti interviewed', *Lyttelton Times*, 29 August 1879.

27   Te Whiti o Rongomai in conversation with S. Croumbie-Brown, Charles Wallace translator, 'Among the Maoris in the North Island', *The Star*, 3 September 1879.

28   Hazel Riseborough, *Days of Darkness: The Government and Parihaka Taranaki 1878–1884* (rev. edn), Penguin, Auckland, 2002, pp.19–20.

29   After Parihaka was invaded, the homes of Māori who did not support Parihaka and who had, in fact, fought on the side of the Crown in the first Taranaki wars were invaded and ransacked too. See Rachel Buchanan, *The Parihaka Album: Lest We Forget*, Huia, Wellington, 2009, pp.86–87.

30   Cited in ibid., pp.43–44.

31   Charge Book – January 1878-October 1884, ADUW 17906 P-NP4/1, ANZ.

Chapter 3

1   Email Richard Hill and Sherwood Young to Rachel

Buchanan, 4 April 2018. Both men were members of the police delegation that went to Parihaka in 1981. At the time, Inspector Young was ministerial services officer, the Police Headquarters liaison officer in the office of the Minister of Police, Ben Couch. Hill (now a professor at Victoria University) was working on a history of nineteenth-century policing in New Zealand, a project instigated by Young.

2   Email Richard Hill and Sherwood Young to Rachel Buchanan, 4 April 2018.

3   'Arohamai remember Parihaka 5th November 1881' reads the front of the T-shirt, on sale in Taranaki in 2010. With thanks to Honiana Love for this reference, the T-shirt and all the other tautoko.

4   See Buchanan, 'Dementia Wing', in *The Parihaka Album: Lest We Forget*, Huia, Wellington, 2009, pp.203–34. The dementia wing at Village at the Park is named after my grandmother, Rawinia Buchanan, in recognition of almost fifty years of service as assistant secretary of the Wellington Rugby Football Union. In this role, Flossie (as she insisted we call her)

controlled seating allocation at Athletic Park, among other things.

5   Richard Hill, 'War and Police: The Armed Constabulary in the Taranaki Wars', in Day (ed.), *Contested Ground Te Whenua I Tohea: The Taranaki Wars 1860–1881*, Huia, Wellington, 2010, p.205.

6   Roberto Rabel, 'New Zealand's Wars', in Giselle Byrnes (ed.), *New Oxford History of New Zealand*, Oxford University Press, Melbourne, 2010, p.245.

7   Dion Tuuta, 'Perpetual Leasing in Taranaki, 1860–1881', in Richard Boast and Richard Hill (eds), *Raupatu: The Confiscation of Māori Land*, Victoria University Press, Wellington, 2009, pp.235–42.

8   See Buchanan, 'Orimupiko 22 and the Haze of History', pp.66–78; Rachel Buchanan, 'Where Did Orimupiko 22 Come From?', unpublished paper prepared at the request of Dr Leo Buchanan and presented to Orimupiko 22 Ahu Whenua Trust hui, May 2016, Pataka, Porirua.

9   Te Miringa Hōhaia, 'The Foundation Story', *Te Maunga Taranaki*, Govett-Brewster Art Gallery, New Plymouth, 2001, p.15. See Nga Iwi O Taranaki and The Crown, Te Anga

Pūtakerongo mō Ngā Maunga o Taranaki, Pouākai me Kaitake, 20 December 2017, www.beehive.govt.nz/release/landmark-day-taranaki-maunga (accessed 23 May 2018). See also 'Maoris Angry over Gifting of Mt Egmont', *Taranaki Herald*, 25 June 1979, p.1.

10   Dennis Ngāwhare-Pounamu, 'Living Memory and the Travelling Mountain Narrative of Taranaki', PhD thesis, Victoria University of Wellington, 2014, p.28.

11   *The Taranaki Report: Kaupapa Tuatahi*, Waitangi Tribunal, Wellington, 1996, p. 312. The paragraph reads: 'As to quantum, the gravamen of our report has been to say that the Taranaki claims are likely to be the largest in the country. The graphic muru of most of Taranaki and the raupatu without ending describe the holocaust of Taranaki history and the denigration of the founding peoples in a continuum from 1840 to the present.'

12   Ngāti Mutunga and Her Majesty the Queen in right of New Zealand, *Deed of Settlement of the Historical Claims of Ngati Mutunga*, 31 July 2008. The waiata, 'Te Whakamā', is in the Historical Account section, p.44.

13   Judith Binney, 'History and Memory: The Wood of the Whau Tree, 1766–2005', in Byrnes (ed.), *The New Oxford History of New Zealand*, p.74.

14   Email Te Miringa Hōhaia to Rachel Buchanan, 7 December 2009.

15   Janna Thompson, 'Is Apology a Sorry Affair? Derrida and the Moral Force of the Impossible', *The Philosophical Forum*, 41, 3 (2010), pp.259–74.

16   Janna Thompson, 'Apology, Justice and Respect: A Critical Defence of Political Apology', in Mark Gibney, Rhoda E. Howard-Hassman, Jean Marc Coicaud and Niklaus Steiner (eds), *Age of Apology Facing Up To The Past*, University of Pennsylvania Press, Philadelphia, 2008, pp.40–42.

17   Douglas Graham, 'Iwi o Taranaki', statement from Office of the Minister of Justice, delivered by Tom Winitana on 17 October 1991 at Parihaka, see Record of Inquiry, Taranaki Report, F17 (a) 3, Waitangi Tribunal Archive (hereafter WTA).

18   Te Miringa Hōhaia (Milton Hōhaia), letter to the Minister of Justice, re: Apology for Parihaka, 27 February 1992,

Taranaki Report, Record of Inquiry, F17 (b), WTA.

19 Douglas Graham to Hōhaia, 9 April 1992, F17 c, WTA.

20 These deeds and all the others are available on the Office of Treaty Settlements website by searching under the iwi name. Go to www.govt.nz/treaty-settlement-documents/ (accessed 18 July 2018).

21 Peter Adds, 'Te Muru me te Raupatu: The Aftermath', in Day (ed.), *Contested Ground*, p. 271.

22 See, especially, Hana Te Hemara, 'Statement by Te Atiawa Women in Support of Taranaki Raupatu Claims', 9 April 1991, Documents to the end of the fourth hearing, D10, WTA.

23 J.C. Sturm, 'There Was a Man', in Hōhaia, O'Brien and Strongman (eds), *Parihaka: The Art of Passive Resistance*, p.205.

24 See Ngā Iwi O Taranaki and The Crown, Te Anga Pūtakerongo mō Ngā Maunga o Taranaki, Pouākai me Kaitake, 20 December 2017, www.beehive.govt.nz/release/landmark-day-taranaki-maunga (accessed 23 May 2018).

25 Christopher Finlayson, 'Parihaka Has Waited a Long Time for This Day', full text of speech and Crown apology published in E-tangata, https://e-tangata.co.nz/history/parihaka-has-waited-a-long-time-for-this-day (accessed 18 July 2018).

26 Te Pire Haeata ki Parihaka/Parihaka Reconciliation Bill, 298-1, www.legislation.govt.nz/bill/government/2017/0298/latest/d56e2.html (accessed 22 May 2018).

Chapter 4

1 Leo Buchanan, The Heaven Project, letter to Lily Arapera Gentile, *c*. July 2017, underlining and capital letters in the original. Dad was paraphrasing lines from Eliot's *Four Quartets*. Quoted with permission of Lily Gentile.

2 Berber Bevernage, *History, Memory, and State-Sponsored Violence*, Routledge, London, 2012, p.ix.

3 This idea of time seeping, infusing and refusing to be boxed up is threaded through Maria Tumakin's *Axiomatic*, Brow Books, Melbourne, 2018, but see, especially, p.128.

4 Buchanan, *The Parihaka Album: Lest We Forget*, Huia, Wellington, 2009, pp.152–56.

5   Lindsay Rihari McLeod, Record of Inquiry from first Parihaka hearing, WTA, F12, p.3.

6   Matt Rilkoff, 'Turning a Page in History', *Taranaki Daily News*, 18 March 2010, p.1.

7   Geoffrey Bagshaw, interviewed by Alexis Wright, *Tracker*, Giramondo, Sydney, 2017, p.203.

8   Tracker Tilmouth, in Wright, *Tracker*, p.447.

9   Joan Metge and Patricia J. Kinloch, *Talking Past Each Other: Problems of Cross-cultural Communication*, Victoria University Press, Wellington, 1978, pp.22–23. With thanks to Neville Gilmour for suggesting this excellent source.

10 Alexis Wright, 'Secrets and Ties', *The Age*, 6 February 2010, A2, pp.12–13.

11 Tracker Tilmouth, in Wright, *Tracker*, p.84.

12 Alice Te Punga Somerville, '"The Historian Who Lost His Memory": A Story About Stories', *Te Pouhere Kōrero*, 3 (2009), p.64. Buck's story is cited as undated. 'Manuscript Notes of Peter H Buck' MS SC BUCK Box 2.29, Bishop Museum, Honolulu, Hawaii.

13 Laura Ann Stoler, *Along the Archival Grain: Epistemic Anxieties and Colonial Common Sense*, Princeton University Press, New Jersey, 2009, pp.248–49. For an analysis of how this works in Australia, see Chris Healy, *Forgetting Aborigines*, UNSW Press, Sydney, 2008.

14 Peter Adds, 'Te Muru', in Kelvin Day (ed.), *Contested Ground Te Whenua I Tohea: The Taranaki Wars 1860–1881*, Huia, Wellington, 2010, p.276.

15 Janna Thompson, *Taking Responsibility for the Past: Reparation and Historical Injustice*, Polity Press, Cambridge, 2002, p.82.

16 Bronwyn Batten, 'The Myall Creek Memorial: History, Identity and Reconciliation', in William Logan and Keir Reeves (eds), *Places of Pain and Shame: Dealing with 'Difficult Heritage'*, Routledge, London, 2009, pp.82–96. See also Jane Lydon and Lyndall Ryan (eds), *Remembering the Myall Creek Massacre*, New South Books, Sydney, 2018.

17 The drum is integral to poi and waiata at Parihaka. For example, see two photographs taken in 1984 (John Miller) and in 1994 (Gil Hanly) at Parihaka. In the second one, Tahuaroa plays the drum. See Hōhaia, O'Brien and

Strongman (eds), *Parihaka: The Art of Passive Resistance*, Victoria University Press, Wellington, 2001, p.85.

18 See, for example, William Collis's photograph of the magnificent 'Parihaka fife and drum band 1880–1890s' outside Te Raukura, Alexander Turnbull Library 1/1-012052-G.

19 'Te Piukara', transcribed and translated by Te Miringa Hōhaia, in Hōhaia, O'Brien and Strongman (eds), *Parihaka: The Art of Passive Resistance*, pp.46–47. A similar point was made by Tamati Whanganui and others in their petition to the New Zealand government in 1925, a petition that was part of the huge push to get an inquiry into confiscated land. Of the invasion day, Whanganui wrote: 'When Te Whiti and Tohu did not surrender to the Government, the Parihaka Pa was besieged by Mr Bryce and his soldiers. Whereat Te Whiti said, "If you shoot me I will surrender, but if your gun does not fire, you will surrender yourself to me."' Tamati Whanganui and others, 'To the Honourable Speaker and Members in Parliament assembled at Wellington',

petition 93/1925, MA 85, 4, Archives New Zealand.

20 Linda Tuhiwai Smith, *Decolonizing Methodologies: Research and Indigenous Peoples*, Otago University Press, Dunedin, 1999, p.34; Dipesh Chakrabarty, *Provincializing Europe: Postcolonial Thought and Historical Difference*, Princeton University Press, New Jersey, 2001.

21 Stephen Turner, 'Settlement as Forgetting', in K. Neumann et al. (eds), *Quicksands: Foundational Histories in Australia & Aotearoa New Zealand*, UNSW Press, Sydney, 1999, p.35.

22 Dr Pita Sharples, cited in Brenda Joyce, Bruce Mathers and Owen Ormsby, *Whakapapa: An Introduction to Researching Māori and Pākehā–Māori Families, Their History, Heritage and Culture*, Māori Interest Group, New Zealand Society of Genealogists, Wellington, 2008, p.4.

23 Arini Loader, 'Casting The Net Wider: Native American Literary Nationalism in Aotearoa', *Te Pouhere Kōrero*, 4 (2010), p.53.

24 Melissa Matutina Williams, *Panguru and the City: Kāinga*

Tahi, Kāinga Rua, Bridget Williams Books, Wellington, 2015.

25   Melissa Williams, 'When It Comes To Your Own: Telling Stories of Post-War Māori Migration', and Nepia Mahuika, 'Kōrero Tuku Iho: Our Gift and Our Responsibility', both in *Te Pouhere Kōrero*, 4 (2010), pp.14–23 and pp.24–40. See also Nepia Mahuika, '"This Horrid Practice": The Cannibalizing of Māori and Iwi History', paper delivered at New Zealand History Association conference, December 2009, for a frank discussion of the place of whakapapa in ethical history-making.

26   Alice Te Punga Somerville, *Once Were Pacific: Māori Connections to Oceania*, University of Minnesota Press, Minneapolis, 2015.

27   Maria Nugent, 'Aboriginal Family History: Some Reflections', *Australian Cultural History*, 22 (2003), p.144.

28   Graeme Davison, *The Use and Abuse of Australian History*, Allen & Unwin, Sydney, 2000, pp.80–109. See also Gary Tippet, 'One Big Family', *Sunday Age*, 31 October 2010.

29   Joy Damousi, 'Why Do We Get So Emotional About Anzac?', in Marilyn Lake and Henry Reynolds (eds), *What's Wrong With Anzac? The Militarisation of Australian History*, New South Books, Sydney, 2010, pp.95–97.

30   Tanya Evans, 'Secrets and Lies: The Radical Potential of Family History', *History Workshop Journal* (Summer 2011), p.36.

31   Helen Harvey, 'Hongi Great Levelling Experience for Archbishop', *Taranaki Herald*, 4 March 2010.

32   'Reader Not Happy with Sir Paul', Connie Jones, letter to the editor, *Taranaki Herald*, 15 March 2010.

33   Tim Ryan, 'The British Army in Taranaki', in Day (ed.), *Contested Ground*, p.126. Ryan describes how British Army solider Philip Walsh, a member of Hatchment – 65th (Yorkshire North Riding), came up with the idea of decorating St Mary's with 'painted memorial hatchments commemorating various regiments'. The first painting was put up in 1878, the last in 1908.

34   Melissa Nobles, *The Politics of Official Apologies*, Cambridge University Press, New York, 2008, p.121.

35   Philip Temple, 'New Book on

Treaty Takes Political Line', *New Zealand Herald*, 15 July 2004, cited in Nobles, *The Politics of Official Apologies*, p.122.

36 A similar claim of Pākehā victimhood is expressed by Dennis Stewart of Ōakura in his letter to the editor, *Taranaki Daily News*, 30 April 2018, 'Strutt Painting a Truth'. Stewart says William Strutt's 1861 painting of 'Maori driving off settler cattle' depicted what happened to some of his ancestors 'who, under threat of attack by Maori, fled from their land at Omata with very little warning insomuch they had to flee for their lives. No time to gather up belongings and herd their stock. So, what they abandoned was there for the taking, looting and burning.'

37 'Historical Account: Sim Commission', Ngāti Mutunga Deed of Settlement, pp.43–44. I also wish to acknowledge the help of Miriama Evans of Ngāti Mutunga, with the translation and interpretation of 'Te Whakamā'. 'Ko Waitara' is on p. 43 of the deed.

38 Thompson, *Taking Responsibility for the Past*, p.47.

39 Waitara 1859–1936, *Souvenir of Pomare Memorial Meeting,* Hui Whakamāhara Ki a Maui Pomare, Manukorihi Pa, Waitara, 27 June 1936, Collection of National Library of Australia.

40 See Rachel Buchanan, https://rachelbuchanan100. com/2015/05/25/te-ra-o-maui-pomare-2013-a-slow-reading/blog post; Patricia O'Brien, *Tautai: Sāmoa, World History and the life of Ta'isi O.F. Nelson*, University of Hawaii Press, Honolulu, 2017; Rachel Buchanan, 'Friendship Can Be a Revolutionary Force', talk delivered 19 August 2017, TATTE Convention Centre, Apia, Sāmoa, www. samoaplanet.com/friendship-can-revolutionary-force (accessed 18 July 2018).

41 Peter Moeahu, 'The Promise of Parihaka', *Taranaki Daily News*, 16 January 2010.

42 Ruakere Hond, 'Pae 9, Te Kawenata/Phase 9, The aspirations of Parihaka'. These are the final two lines of Te Tikanga Tuku Iho Legacy Statement, He Pire Haeata ki Parihaka/Parihaka Reconciliation Bill, 2018.

43 See Claire Trevett, 'Crown Apology, Unique Reconciliation Package Create "New Dawn" for Te Whiti's Parihaka', *New Zealand*

Herald, 9 June 2017. Also 'Apology to Parihaka: "The Crown Responded To Peace With Tyranny"', *New Zealand Herald*, 9 June 2017.

44 See Shannon Haunui-Thompson, 'Tears as Crown Apologies for Parihaka Atrocities', Te Manu Korihi, RNZ, 9 June 2017, www.radionz.co.nz/news/te-manu-korihi/332613/tears-as-crown-apologises-for-parihaka-atrocities (accessed 18 July 2018).

45 A high-profile, Australian-based descendant of John Bryce is Moira Rainer. On 9 June 2017, I noticed that Rainer, a lawyer and human rights activist, was tweeting about Parihaka. I had interviewed Rayner when she was the Commissioner for Equal Opportunity in Victoria in the early 1990s. The state government of the day had wanted to close down the women's prison in Melbourne and co-locate the women with the men in Pentridge. The Commission took legal action against the government to stop this. The plan was scrapped but Rayner's role was also abolished.

46 Te Whiti o Rongomai in conversation with S.

Croumbie-Brown, Charles Wallace translator, 'Among the Maoris in the North Island', *The Star*, 3 September 1879.

Chapter 5

1 See agency 'history and notes' for Department of Corrections, Prison Staff College (ABGU) 1972-current in Archives New Zealand's Archway search engine. With sincere thanks to Hugh Karena, Director Māori Relationships and Strategy at Department of Internal Affairs, and Katrina Tamaira, research archivist, Archives New Zealand, for facilitating quick access to the Prison Register and Charge Book.

2 I owe this observation to Tony Ballantyne who used these two marvellous words to describe the power of certain archives at the 'Critical Archives: New Practices, New Interpretations' conference, Deakin University, Melbourne, 13–14 November 2017.

3 In his PhD thesis, 'Living Memory and the Travelling Mountain Narrative of Taranaki', Dennis Ngāwhare-Pounamu cites Te Kahui Kararehe as one of three Taranaki iwi pūkōrero (primary informant who gave

oral information to Pākehā authors in the nineteenth century). The other two were Taurua Minarapa and Minarapa Kahukura Makuru. The three recipients of traditional histories were ethnographers Stephenson Percy Smith, Elsdon Best and William Skinner.

4   Rigby Allan notes ARC2007-233/1, phrases quoted from Allan's notes in folder 9: 29.12.61; Notes 30 October 1971; Trip to Parihaka 7 November 1956; 7 November 1961, Puke Ariki Museum, New Plymouth.

Chapter 6

1   Alexis Wright, *Tracker*, Giramondo, Sydney, 2017, p.389.

ABOUT THE AUTHOR

Dr Rachel Buchanan (Taranaki, Te Ātiawa) is an historian, archivist, journalist and curator. Rachel is the author of *The Parihaka Album: Lest We Forget* (Huia, 2009) and *Stop Press: The Last Days of Newspapers* (Scribe, 2013). She wrote poems for *The Anatomy Lesson*, an artist book by Geoffrey Ricardo and in 2014 she produced an artist newspaper, *Melbourne Sirius*. Her essays on trees and Taranaki land have been anthologised in *Tell You What: Great New Zealand Non-Fiction* (2015, 2016). Between October 2015 and March 2018, Rachel was curator, Germaine Greer Archive, University of Melbourne Archives. Her essay 'How Shakespeare Helped Shape Germaine Greer's Masterpiece' won a 2016 Australian Society of Archivists Mander Jones award. Rachel has been published in *The Conversation*, *The Monthly*, *Meanjin*, *Griffith Review*, *VICE NZ* and Fairfax newspapers. Her scholarly writing has been translated into Māori, Farsi and French and has appeared in journals in Australia, New Zealand, Canada, Iran and the United States.

About BWB Texts

BWB Texts are short books on big subjects from great New Zealand writers. They are succinct narratives spanning contemporary issues, memoir, history and science. With well over fifty BWB Texts in print and more available digitally, new works are published regularly. BWB Texts can be purchased from all good bookstores and online from www.bwb.co.nz.

BWB Texts include:

A Matter of Fact: Talking Truth in a Post-Truth World
Jess Berentson-Shaw

Better Lives: Migration, Wellbeing and New Zealand
Julie Fry and Peter Wilson

Doing Our Bit: The Campaign to Double the Refugee Quota
Murdoch Stephens

Thought for Food: Why What We Eat Matters
John D. Potter

Island Time: New Zealand's Pacific Futures
Damon Salesa

The Bike and Beyond: Life on Two Wheels in Aotearoa New Zealand
Laura Williamson

Late Love: Sometimes Doctors Need Saving as Much as Their Patients
Glenn Colquhoun

Three Cities: Seeking Hope in the Anthropocene
Rod Oram

Playing for Both Sides: Love Across the Tasman
Stephanie Johnson

Complacent Nation
Gavin Ellis

The First Migration: Māori Origins 3000BC – AD1450
Atholl Anderson

Silencing Science
Shaun Hendy

Going Places: Migration, Economics and the Future of New Zealand
Julie Fry & Hayden Glass

The Interregnum: Rethinking New Zealand
Morgan Godfery (ed)

Christchurch Ruptures
Katie Pickles

Home Truths: Confronting New Zealand's Housing Crisis
Philippa Howden-Chapman

Polluted Inheritance: New Zealand's Freshwater Crisis
Mike Joy

Wealth and New Zealand
Max Rashbrooke

Why Science Is Sexist
Nicola Gaston

Towards a Warmer World: What Climate Change Will Mean for New Zealand's Future
Veronika Meduna

The Edge of Life: Controversies and Challenges in Human Health
Mike Berridge

Out of the Vaipe, the Deadwater: A Writer's Early Life
Albert Wendt

Sugar, Rum and Tobacco: Taxes and Public Health in New Zealand
Mike Berridge and Lisa Marriott

Old Asian, New Asian
K. Emma Ng

Fair Borders? Migration Policy in the Twenty-First Century
David Hall (ed.)

The Whole Intimate Mess: Motherhood, Politics, and Women's Writing
Holly Walker

Tax and Fairness
Deborah Russell and Terry Baucher